Rainbow
STRAIGHT BETWEEN THE EYES

Laura Shenton

"If I had Rainbow to do over again, I'd have more of the band that I have now. The overall sound of Rainbow is coming out better on this album."

— *Ritchie Blackmore, May 1982*

"This is an album that should appeal to everyone. What we've done on this album is strike a balance between the accessibility of the last few albums and the progressivism of the earlier ones. This is unquestionably the most diverse album that Rainbow's ever done, and I believe it's the best as well. It's the type of music that we've been trying to make for a long time."

— *Roger Glover, April 1982*

"Ritchie had this vision of Rainbow becoming a commercial rock band. He was living in the States at the time, and I remember him saying: 'I want to hear my songs on American radio.' We knew exactly what we were doing."

— *Joe Lynn Turner, 2005*

Rainbow
STRAIGHT BETWEEN THE EYES

Laura Shenton

WP
WYMER
PUBLISHING
Bedford, England

First published in 2022 by Wymer Publishing
Bedford, England www.wymerpublishing.co.uk Tel: 01234 326691
Wymer Publishing is a trading name of Wymer (UK) Ltd

Copyright © 2022 Laura Shenton / Wymer Publishing. This edition published 2022.

Print edition (fully illustrated): **ISBN: 978-1-912782-96-3**

Edited by Jerry Bloom.

The Author hereby asserts her rights to be identified as the author of this work in accordance with sections 77 to 78 of the Copyright, Designs & Patents Act 1988.

All rights reserved. No part of this publication may be reproduced or transmitted in any form or by any means, electronic or mechanical, including photocopying, or any information storage and retrieval system, without written permission from the publisher.

This publication is sold subject to the condition that it shall not, by way of trade or otherwise, be lent, re-sold, hired out or otherwise circulated without the publishers' prior consent in any form of binding or cover other than that in which it is published and without a similar condition including this condition being imposed on the subsequent purchaser.

eBook formatting by Coinlea.
Printed and bound in Great Britain by
CMP, Dorset.

A catalogue record for this book is available from the British Library.

Typeset by Andy Bishop / 1016 Sarpsborg
Cover design by 1016 Sarpsborg.
Cover photo © Pictorial Press / Alamy Stock Photo

Contents

Preface   7

Chapter One: Why Straight Between The Eyes?   9

Chapter Two: The Making of Straight Between The Eyes   31

Chapter Three: Live Between The Eyes   55

Chapter Four: Legacy   81

Discography   101

Tour Dates   105

Preface

I find it infinitely fascinating to consider that when *Straight Between The Eyes* was released in 1982, a lot of Rainbow fans weren't all too pleased about it. For fans who were around at the time, there was a lot of apprehension towards Rainbow as soon as the band had made a deliberate departure from the sound that many had come to love when Ronnie James Dio was on vocals. And it's completely understandable. After having been spellbound by the likes of 'Stargazer' on *Rainbow Rising*, expectations must have been high even after the album that followed it, *Long Live Rock 'n' Roll*.

I was born in 1988 so evidently, I wasn't around when people had those doubts about Rainbow. I didn't live through the frustrations of "their new stuff is nothing like *Rainbow Rising*." In that regard, truthfully, I would suspect that my opinion of the Graham Bonnet and indeed Joe Lynn Turner eras of Rainbow have a bias that is slanted towards the advantage of looking at things retrospectively. I didn't even live through the excitement of the announcement that Deep Purple mark two were due to reunite!

On the basis of the above, you could be thinking, "who is Miss Shenton anyway and why has she written this book?" Well, it's a fair question and as such, I am keen to take this opportunity to promise you that throughout the narrative, I have endeavoured to be objective by referring to what was said at the time about *Straight Between The Eyes* rather than jumping to a whole host of conclusions based on my own bias. So yes, *I* feel that *Straight Between The Eyes* is an amazing album — both in terms of being some damn good melodic rock and in terms of how it offers an insight into where Rainbow were at with things at the time — but all the same, I will certainly make lots of reference to what *other people* said about the album when it was released. It matters — not just in terms of objectivity but in the name of historical accuracy.

1982 was a tentative period for Rainbow; although the line-up of Ritchie Blackmore, Roger Glover, Bobby Rondinelli, Joe Lynn Turner and David Rosenthal all spoke of how happily and how well they were working together, it wouldn't be long before a multitude of factors would see Blackmore put the band on the backburner.

This book is a gossip-free zone. I want to present facts rather than all kinds of weird and wonderful speculations. Also, there will be nothing herein that is in the lexicon of "this song is in B minor so it probably means XYZ". Nope! Not happening! Also, as someone who has no affiliation with Rainbow or with any of their associates, in writing this book, I have ensured to quote good, reliable sources that will help to get the story of *Straight Between The Eyes* across with as much authenticity as possible. Due to this, you'll be seeing lots of quotes from vintage articles. I think they are important to document anyway because there will probably come a time when stuff like that gets harder to source.

Chapter One

Why Straight Between The Eyes?

Released in April 1982, *Straight Between The Eyes* is perhaps one of the more overlooked Rainbow albums. Sure, it got to number five in the UK and to number thirty in the US. And yes, it met the objectives of Ritchie Blackmore's aim to be more commercial by that point. But with the Ronnie James Dio era of Rainbow being so far in the past by that point, it is understandable as to why at the time, Rainbow's sixth studio album was vulnerable to falling under the radar of many rock fans. But really, *Straight Between The Eyes* documents an era in which Rainbow were working well together. They all said as much across a number of interviews, as this book will show. Joe Lynn Turner was no longer the new guy. Having established himself with the band by filling in on the songs that had originally been written for Graham Bonnet's vocals on *Difficult To Cure* (1981), rapport, confidence and creativity within the band was at a high point.

The Dio era Rainbow albums had been recorded and released between 1975 and 1978 (*Ritchie Blackmore's Rainbow* (1975), *Rainbow Rising* (1976) and *Long Live Rock 'n' Roll* (1978)). When Ronnie Dio had left the band, it came with further line-up changes and saw Don Airey join on keyboards (he had played with Cozy Powell's Hammer previously — Powell had been in Rainbow since 1975) along with Roger Glover on bass and Graham Bonnet on vocals. It could be said that Bonnet was a surprising choice of vocalist for Rainbow in view of how with his previous band, the Marbles, hard rock hadn't been the order of the day. Apparently Bonnet aced the audition for Rainbow though. According to rumour, Blackmore and co. were keen to give him the job after he'd sung just the first few notes of the Deep Purple song, 'Mistreated'.

With Bonnet on vocals, the resulting album was *Down To Earth*. It signified a clear change in style. Dio era mythical lyrics and medieval inspired themes were out and a more commercial sound was in. *Down To Earth* features many songs on the theme of love and women — a far cry from the likes of 'Sixteenth Century Greensleeves' and 'Gates Of Babylon'.

It was a surprise to many Rainbow fans in 1979 to find that *Down To Earth* features the Russ Ballard-penned song, 'Since You Been Gone'. The song had previously been covered by all girl band, Clout. Despite Rainbow's rock treatment of the song, on paper and in the grand scheme of things, it was certainly a new direction in comparison to expectations that had been set by a song like 'Stargazer' on *Rainbow Rising*.

The change in direction on *Down To Earth* was no accident though; Blackmore had made the decision to target his music more towards the US market. The pop music influence was done with the view to getting radio play. And of course, more radio play means more record sales. It was a reasonable and understandable decision considering that Blackmore was funding Rainbow out of his own pocket. Equally understandable though is the fact that Rainbow's change in direction cost them a number of fans who had enjoyed the band's previous albums.

Roger Glover had been brought on board initially because Blackmore wanted him to offer his talents as a producer. It made sense though for Glover to contribute bass — he was good at it and he and Blackmore had worked well together before in Deep Purple between 1969 and 1973. Not only that, but Glover's skills as a songwriter and arranger brought something positive to the band. Time would show that Glover was an excellent choice — he would go on to contribute significantly to not just *Down To Earth*, but *Difficult To Cure* (1981), *Straight Between The Eyes* (1982) and *Bent Out Of Shape* (1983).

It was considered in *Kerrang!*; "Rainbow, to all intents and purposes, is Blackmore's band. Aside from being the focal point onstage, he supplies the initial musical input on all the songs, determines the fate of group members and, up until the recording of the '79 album *Down To Earth*, was responsible for the band's direction in the studio as well. In the wake of the turmoil, bad feeling and general lack of inspiration that blighted the recording of *Long Live Rock 'n' Roll*, the preceding LP, Ritchie decided he could no longer cope on his own and, after consulting with manager Bruce Payne, asked Roger Glover to join first as producer and additionally as bassist. On *Down To Earth* the final decision in the studio was his, an arrangement that's remained intact on both *Difficult To Cure* and the new *Straight Between The Eyes*."

After doing the promotional touring for *Down To Earth*, another change of line-up was due. Cozy Powell left Rainbow mainly due to how the stylistic change in the band wasn't to his preference — he had made it clear even at the time that he wanted to stick with the heavier style of music that had made the Dio era of the band so endearing to their many fans.

Powell's last performance with Rainbow was at the Monsters Of Rock Festival on 16th August 1980. Bobby Rondinelli — the American drummer who had previously played in a band by the name of Samantha and ended up replacing Powell in Rainbow — was present at the gig.

Blackmore, Glover, Airey, Bonnet and Rondinelli went to Sweet Silence Studios in Copenhagen to get to work on the next LP. However, a lack of good rapport between Bonnet and Blackmore resulted in the vocalist leaving the band. Inconveniently, Bonnet's departure from Rainbow was partway through the recording of what was to become *Difficult To Cure*. As a result, Rainbow were left in the lurch until they were able to find a replacement in Joe Lynn Turner.

Turner said of how he came to be in Rainbow; "I got a phone call from Barry Ambrosia... Barry was Ritchie's personal assistant in Long Island. He was a fan of Fandango. He told Ritchie to come see me sing. Months before the band had broke up Ritchie came to a show. Well, months later I got a call and Barry asked me if I had heard of Rainbow. The only album I had owned was *Rainbow Rising*. Barry goes, 'I am sitting next to Ritchie Blackmore.' I said, 'Put him on.' I hear this guy say, 'Hello mate.' I said, 'Is this really Ritchie Blackmore? Who is this? Is this one of my friends pulling my leg? You know what kind of state I am in. This is really not funny.' This guy goes, 'What state are you talking about? You're in New York, aren't you?' I knew that was a really innocent answer and I knew then this was really him. Ritchie said, 'I am a fan of yours and I want you to come down and audition for Rainbow'."

And of his audition; "I had a terrible cold but I needed the work. I wasn't sure how big Rainbow was or wasn't. I got directions on which train to take out of the city and to Kingdom Sound in Long Island. Ritchie's tour manager picked me up at the station. I walked in and there Ritchie was with Amy, his third wife. Roger Glover was at the boards and I just said hello. They literally pushed me into the studio and go, 'We are going to play you a track. Can you make up sounds? Just syllables or something?' I said, 'Let me hear the track.' I reached into what Ritchie later called my Magic Bag and began shuffling through my lyrics. I found one that kind of fit the groove and I started singing these melodies and lyrics. They shut the track off and they are all in the studio behind the glass. There is dead silence and I was like a goldfish in a bowl. They said, 'Here is another one' and they did the same thing. After that they said, 'Here is one that is already pretty much done' and they played 'I Surrender' with Graham Bonnet on it. They said, 'Can you mimic that?' and I said 'No, but I can sing it my way.' The end result was that we brushed it up a bit but we knew we were never going to get any publishing from Russ Ballad, the guy who wrote the song. The version that made it onto the record is actually different than the demo. It is not a whole lot different but it did make it better. I started singing the song and I started stacking the vocals on it. I was thinking, 'What's going on here?' Finally, Ritchie came in with a six-pack of Heinekens and said, 'Do you want the job?' I said yes. Ritchie goes, 'You're in. Now get to work.' They didn't even let me go back to New York City to get some clothes. They took me to a department store and I bought some jeans and sweatshirts. They put me in the Burt Bacharach Hotel and that is where we wrote 'Freedom Fighter' and all of those songs."

When it came to establishing himself as a member of Rainbow, Turner had his work cut out. Although he had already proven himself with his band Fandango, having made four studio albums and done the associated promotional tours, the fact that the songs for *Difficult To Cure* had been written for Bonnet's voice meant that there were some challenges in terms of having to fill another musician's shoes. A lot of the backing tracks had already been recorded with Bonnet in mind and it meant that Turner had to sing in a higher key than he would have preferred.

Although having to fill in where Bonnet had taken off, Turner brought with him an enthusiasm for the songs he was asked to do. The way in which Bonnet and Turner both had a different approach to working was apparent during the recording of 'No Release'. Blackmore told *Kerrang!* in April 1982; "I'd written the music to it and I said well, it's just a blues — it's up to the singer what he does. I could go into what Graham said but I won't. Then Joe came along and went 'oh yeah, I'll sing that' and came up with his own tune. It was great, it just worked straight away. I still don't like the tune particularly, it's all right, but he did a great job with a bit of a throwaway song."

Difficult To Cure was released in February 1981. It got to number three in the UK and to number fifty in the US. The iconic cover art was made by Hipgnosis, famed for having already worked with Pink Floyd, The Nice, Wishbone Ash, Renaissance and Emerson, Lake and Palmer (to name just a few!). In fact the artwork was originally prepared but rejected for Black Sabbath's 1978 album *Never Say Die*.

Even before the album was released, there was perhaps a sense that it wasn't as good as it could be. Glover told *Kerrang!*; "When *Difficult To Cure* was finished I went through terrible nervous breakdowns wondering if it sounded right and just before it came out I was shitting bricks. I didn't think it was good enough. *Difficult To Cure* I thought was basically a good album but I was worried about the sound. I couldn't put my finger on it but there was something about it I didn't like, a certain clarity that wasn't there. I wanted to re-do it completely. About a week before it was due out I was calling up our manager saying 'can I re-mix it? I really think I can do better' and he's going 'no, it'll cost too much money'." Later on though, Glover told *Cleveland Scene* in May 1982; "I'm still proud of *Down To Earth* and *Difficult To Cure*."

Geoff Barton reviewed *Difficult To Cure* for *Sounds* in February 1981; "TWO STARS?! I hear you scream. Yes, I'm afraid so. To come straight to the point and with the minimum of waffle: the days when a new Rainbow album was automatically awarded a *Sounds* "Indispensable" tag are over. Finished. Dead and gone. I'm not taking this slant simply to be controversial. I'm not about to give *Difficult To Cure* a drubbing because I feel it's an "interesting" or "different" angle to adopt. No, I sincerely believe that this LP is desperately disappointing, and moreover that guitarist and band leader Ritchie Blackmore has had his day. I've said it. And I've started, so I'll finish."

Bonnet's and drummer Cozy Powell's departures from Rainbow heralded yet another new beginning for the band. However, despite criticisms of Mr Blackmore's continual chopping and changing of the group line-up, Barton argued that the multifarious Rainbow "developments" had generally worked out for the best. Indeed it was Blackmore's prerogative to make changes to his own band after all, and indeed more often than not it could be argued that his (initially apparently arbitrary) alterations had worked spectacularly well. Bonnet for example, despite his rather smooth appearance, was a more than worthy successor to Ronnie James Dio. Similarly, Roger Glover was a wise choice to hold down the position of bassist and Don Airey was a strong choice of keyboard player.

But as Barton saw it, the album signified that Blackmore's once unerring ability to choose the right musicians was beginning to wane. The critic particularly regarded new drummer Bobby Rondinelli as "less than forceful, languishing at the back of the mix and making little impact, a sorry substitute for pounding Powell power." And of the singer he said, "shrill voiced Joe Lynn Turner has none of Bonnet's commanding vocal presence, spending far too much time apeing Foreigner's Lou Gramm for comfort."

Barton concluded that "the new Rainbow is not better, nor even as good as the old. For the first time, it's worse. Coincidentally, Blackmore's playing seems to be suffering as well. Late on in his career, he seems content to limit himself to the "hit singles market" rather than branch out into new areas of axepertise. In fact, his playing on *Difficult To Cure* sounds terribly slow and dated. Apart from the odd classical take-off, the guitar tracks could conceivably have been recorded around Deep Purple's *Machine Head* days. While the new breed of guitar hero — the likes of Eddie Van Halen, Alex Lifeson and Randy Hansen — breaks new ground it's sad, not to say tragic, that the once masterful Blackmore has been left behind. He quite happily ploughs old furrows and steadfastly refuses to move with the times."

Barton was a widely respected journalist at the time and he said of the top three hit 'I Surrender'; "The Russ Ballard song Blackmore filched from Praying Mantis. Lord knows why the guitarist went to such great lengths to secure the number as it is, at best, a poor man's 'Hold The Line'. That said, it's nonetheless preferable to a version of the Shirelles' 'Will You Love Me Tomorrow', once mooted as 'the next Rainbow single' and even performed at Castle Donington. But only just."

Of 'Spotlight Kid' he said Blackmore's lead breaks sounded hackneyed and the Cossack dancing/ELP-style mid-section was confusing and incongruous.

Bizarrely he saw 'No Release' as a Led Zeppelin style number and 'Magic' as lightweight American top forty material.

Even the excellent instrumental, 'Vielleicht Das Nachster Zeit (Maybe Next Time)' was dismissed as an introspective slow bluesy piece that would probably have been labelled "tasteful" in the early seventies; in Barton's view, it sounded time-warped. "If Rik Emmett started playing this you'd shout 'Rubbish!' For heaven's sake Ritchie, this is 1981," cried Barton.

'Can't Happen Here' he saw as being given the supreme limp-wristed treatment. He also complained that the pivotal guitar riff sounded naggingly familiar. On that he was correct; it's the same as the one on Little Richard's 1956 song 'The Girl Can't Help It'.

Even 'Freedom Fighter', which Barton saw as one of the album's better tracks, was criticised for Joe Lynn Turner's homogenised AOR vocals not fitting comfortably with the rough 'n' tumble subject matter.

'Midtown Tunnel Vision' was described as being like a track from an early Robin Trower LP. And finally, Barton regarded 'Difficult To Cure', as a disastrous instrumental.

Notably, Barton's review of *Down To Earth* had also been pretty disparaging too with comments like "While on one hand the band must be commended for keeping matters short and simple on this album (no meandering three-and-a-half hour versions of 'Catch The Rainbow' for instance) I nonetheless feel myself pining for the days of yore, when even the band's more basic tracks such as 'Starstruck' and 'Long Live Rock 'n' Roll' had an epic feel, were much more than mere rollicking good-time, four minute throwaways" and "The new Rainbow incarnation has a lot to recommend it; similarly this album is definitely 'worth listening to'... but in these days of the £5 album is it truly worth buying? After infinitely careful consideration I can't bring myself to award it more than three stars. That should tell the tale."

One would suspect that he was in that camp of people who were immensely pissed off that Rainbow had changed direction from the music that was being made with Ronnie Dio in the band. He certainly wasn't the only one though.

As *New Musical Express* put it that month: "Heavy metal is so tame and listless because it is cheap. Pretty music tarted up with hygienically overproduced guitars... Ritchie Blackmore on the Rainbow album hangs conspicuously low, his opportunities to show off saved for the instrumentals which round off each side: 'Vielleicht Das Nachster Zeit (Maybe Next Time)' on side one and a horrendous arrangement of the famous bit from Beethoven's Ninth on side two. Other than these, a few bursts from his time-honoured Stratocaster, either phased or switched between speakers would seem to have appeased the old axe complex. Rainbow make the fatal mistake of including two songs, Russ Ballard's 'I Surrender' and Brian Moran's 'Magic', that wouldn't look amiss in the repertoire, say, of The Dooleys. What this kind of error does for their credibility I don't know. I don't suppose anyone will notice. But it is the barefaced prettiness of such things which as I say, gives the game away."

Kerrang!, renowned for their love of rock and metal and very much championing the genre at the time, were not as disparaging of Rainbow's change of direction towards the more commercial when they reviewed *Difficult To Cure*: "Since the band's inception in '75 Rainbow's line-up has been, to say the least, fluid. With the exception naturally of ex-Purple axeman Ritchie Blackmore, members have come and gone at a steady rate though it must be pointed out that change, however drastic, has usually been for the better, something indeed that still looks true today. The band that crafted last year's *Down To Earth* LP — Cozy Powell (drums), Graham Bonnet (vocals), Roger Glover (bass), Don Airey (keyboards) and the man in black himself on guitar — certainly had a definitive feel but the going of Powell and Bonnet and the coming of Americans Bobby Rondinelli and Joe Lynn Turner has led to no apparent loss in direction of power."

"Rondinelli, like his predecessor, uses his sticks to really force the pace whilst Turner, with a delivery pitched just on the tight-trousered side of Foreigner's Lou Gramm, looks to already have a place in the heavy metal howlers hall of fame. Indeed, on the evidence of this, Rainbow's sixth LP, the present Anglo/US alliance could well be the pot of gold Blackmore's been searching for. To many, of course, *Rainbow Rising* represents the cream of the man's post-Purple forays but in those early formative days the band seemed to be striving just too hard for the epic whereas now they're altogether more confident, relaxed and, above all, musical. Seekers of cerebral cremation may well find this shift disappointing and Roger Glover's production does certainly provide *Difficult To Cure* with a spotless commercial finish but for my money it's the band's most convincing album to date with Blackmore displaying a restraint and economy rarely heard before."

"First away is the current chart single 'I Surrender', an infectious Russ Ballard number boosted by Blackmore's pleading pliant guitar, closely followed by 'Spotlight Kid', an energetic insight into the initially luring yet ultimately fickle world of rock 'n' roll superstardom with Rondinelli's boisterous backbeat tempered by trilling pompy keyboards and just so harmonies. 'No Release' then heralds a more adventurous turn with its coarse-ground bluesy riff giving way to a gospelish mid-section whilst 'Magic', an immaculately handled Brian Moran composition, and 'Vielleicht Das Nachster Zeit (Maybe Next Time)', a poignant pining

Rainbow - *Straight Between The Eyes*: In-depth

instrumental, round off the side in harmonious fashion. A tough first half to match but side two, although marginally weaker, is certainly no poor relation. 'Can't Happen Here' may have a riff similar to that which powered 'All Night Long' but needle-sharp lyrics and expert phrasing make it more than worthwhile whilst one notch up stands 'Freedom Fighter', a superbly arranged rocker with Blackmore supplying both snaking lead and growling solo. 'Midtown Tunnel Vision' is next, the album's heaviest number boasting a measured riff that cardboard guitarists everywhere will soon be making their own. Then it's into the home straight for the title track, a semi-serious cover of a Beethoven opus clearly showing that the links between the heavy and classical music extend. At their best, both combine excitement and emotional appeal with a healthy dash of the epic and that's a mix *Difficult To Cure* achieves to a tee. Ludwig I'm sure would have been proud."

Difficult To Cure was reviewed in *Melody Maker*; "In the eyes of the media Ritchie Blackmore can do nothing right. Inevitably, the new Rainbow album will spark a caustic critical reaction, full of personal attacks about Blackmore's character and his inability to hold a band together. With this in mind, let it be recorded that *Difficult To Cure* is, to these ears, a mighty fine LP, a varied package of hard rock that should delight Rainbow devotees yet attract fresh fans. It comprises nine new songs, delivered with an abundance of energy and skill, opening with the current single 'I Surrender', though I do have some reservations about this track — like 'Since You Been Gone' written by Russ Ballard, and a predictably bouncy tune clearly aimed at the singles market. Fair enough. After their chart success in the past eighteen months, the move toward commercialism is valid, and if the band can come up with good heavy pop songs that retain a hard edge then they can't be accused of mellowing. But why choose another Russ Ballard song? It invites immediate criticism. Ritchie and Roger Glover are capable of penning good pop songs as 'All Night Long' proved and as 'Can't Happen Here' does on this album. 'Spotlight Kid' is the next track, a Blackmore/Glover composition that drives along with great impact. Amid some heroic hard rock riffing Ritchie delivers some slick guitar work, and you're already very aware of the presence of new vocalist Joe Lynn Turner, who took over from Graham Bonnet halfway through the recording of the album. In technique he may not match his predecessor, who had an incredible range, but in general he fits in far better with the group and has also helped Roger out with lyrics or a couple of tunes, something Bonnet never attempted."

"The other new man, drummer Bobby Rondinelli, plays with brilliant control, providing solid skin beating throughout. 'No Release', with hints of Zeppelin, is the most forceful track on side one, with Ritchie playing some of his best lead in years. The song builds gradually, through a slickly-produced vocal break, before exploding with some vicious solo axe. Rainbow have never broken through in a big way in the States and songs like 'Magic' are included to crack the US market; 'Magic' is a refreshing hard rock song, crystal clear and emphasising the strength of Roger Glover's production. However, 'Vielleicht Das Nachster Zeit (Maybe Next Time)', is a slow instrumental dominated by Blackmore's guitar. The second side opens with 'Can't Happen Here', a fast-flowing number that should definitely be released as a single. The riff is reminiscent of 'All Night Long' but the band's attack is given greater punch by Turner's powerful singing. The tempo drops dramatically for 'Midtown Tunnel Vision', a slow blues that bites hard in Hendrix/Zeppelin style, and stands out as the album's killer punch. The album closes with

Rainbow - *Straight Between The Eyes*: In-depth

the title track, another instrumental that is based loosely on Beethoven's Ninth Symphony. Blackmore will doubtless get some stick for using the great composer's theme as a rock piece, but he and Don Airey are in splendid form and fans of the band will recall parts of the number from the Rainbow live show. There is even a touch of humour at the end as the sound of howling laughter (Oliver Hardy, by the way) breaks out when the music stops. *Difficult To Cure* is Rainbow's best album since *Rainbow Rising* and proves that the one and a half year gap since the last studio album has definitely been worth the wait."

Although not all reviews of *Difficult To Cure* were glowing, if the main aim of the album was to get through to a US audience, reviews from that side of the pond would certainly point towards a goal that had been met.

Billboard reviewed the album in March 1981; "There's nothing new on this set by Ritchie Blackmore, Roger Glover and company but the eleven songs here are just what the doctor ordered for many heavy metal fans. The songs have the anthem quality of the best heavy metal songs and Blackmore's guitar work is full of spark as usual."

As did *Cash Box*; "AOR's fever for classic heavy metal is *Difficult To Cure*, but Ritchie Blackmore's latest assemblage of Rainbow delivers the right serum on its newest LP. Led by bassist/producer Roger Glover and Deep Purple's noted blackbeard of guitar (Blackmore), the band tears into a collection filled with break-neck paced rockers topped by 'Can't Happen Here' and 'Spotlight Kid'. Lead singer Joe Lynn Turner is perhaps the finest vocalist to stand with Blackmore since Ian Gillan. Heavy metal blues can be heard in all its glory on 'Midtown Tunnel Vision'."

Overall, *Difficult To Cure* features an abundance of strong tracks — 'I Surrender' and 'Spotlight Kid' as well as the title track. Things were looking up for Rainbow as they set off on a promotional tour. In the March and April of 1981, Rainbow toured America, sharing the bill with the Pat Travers Band. Although Rainbow was being met with a mixed reception by this point in their tenure due to having changed direction commercially and for still being on tentative ground overall, the gig reviews certainly showed that the band had potential and importantly, were enthusiastically welcomed by those who were appreciative of them.

A short break from touring in May provided Roger Glover with the opportunity to begin work on a solo album prior to the start of the European leg of Rainbow's tour. It would see them perform in the UK in July. A lack of London dates drew some criticism but overall, things went well.

A seemingly happy camper, Blackmore's playing on stage was inspired. Supported by a band who gave him what it was he wanted at the time, he even decided to bring the much-requested 'Smoke On The Water' back into the setlist having been encouraged to do so by an enthusiastic Glover and Turner.

'Smoke On The Water' came to be used as encore material spontaneously and after Blackmore had been doubtful about doing it. Turner told *Kerrang!*; "We'd been fooling around with the song in rehearsals and Bobby and I went 'Ritchie, it's great, let's do it' but he kept saying 'no, I left that behind long ago'. Then one night, I forget exactly where, he started the riff on the encore and we just turned round, looked at each other and went 'right!'. The drums and the bass came in and we did it with smiles on our faces from ear to ear, we were bustin' a gut and the people went crazy. I think that's fine, we should do it now and again. I mean that's the legend, why fucking not?"

Cleveland Scene reported in May 1982; "Gone are the

days when Blackmore would piss off audiences by refusing to play his older Deep Purple songs, and although they are not an integral part of Rainbow's set, they are, at least, not as taboo as they used to be." To which Glover was quoted; "I remember the first tour I did with Rainbow. Ritchie absolutely refused to do any Deep Purple songs. Then I think it was the last tour, we brought it up in rehearsals, and he said, 'No'. Then one night in Denver he suddenly started playing it. I think the reason he decided to do it was that Rainbow had become enough of a separate entity where the two didn't combine."

Preparing to perform live with Rainbow had been a new challenge for Turner. In Fandango he had been on guitar half the time on stage and had never toured outside of America and Canada. In terms of his stage presence, it took a little bit of fine tuning and encouragement from Blackmore to get him to where he needed to be for Rainbow.

Blackmore told *Kerrang!* in April 1982; "I know he'll forgive me for saying this, but Joe was still into a bit of a cabaret type act. I had to pull him one night and say you don't do that in Britain, you don't jump around the stage and go crazy, because if you do the kids won't believe what you're singing. I tried to quieten him down which I did after the third date."

Turner told *Kerrang!*; "One night while Bobby was doing his solo, Ritchie came running round the back of the stage and went 'what the hell are you doing?!'. He was right to shout, I was really overstepping the mark. I had the guitar over my head, I was twisting it about and throwing picks out to the audience. I used to do all that stuff and it's hard to break old habits, but there I was doing it with the greatest guitar player in the world going 'oh shit, I've got myself in hot water this time'." ('Difficult To Cure' was the only Rainbow number for which Turner used the guitar on stage).

Rainbow's image, and indeed their audience, went in a different direction with the addition of Turner to the band. He told *Kerrang!* in April 1982; "Well, before it was like celibacy, all geezers. But now we get these sixteen-year-old honeys walking in all feathered up, and really they're taking their lives in their hands. Our stagehands often have to douse the people at the front with water to stop them passing out and you get a girl in that situation and she's just not going to cope. But in Japan they all sit there and get up when they're supposed to and if they make one false move they've got like ninety Ninjas on them. It's complete control."

It was after the tour for *Difficult To Cure* that *Straight Between The Eyes* comes into the picture and indeed, another line-up change.

With the tour concluding in Japan, the flight back to America was broken up by a stopover in Hawaii. Although this was essentially a well-earned break in one of Blackmore's favourite holiday destinations. A low-key concert was also performed at the Andrews Amphitheatre on 5th September and it would prove to be Don Airey's last with the band. Approximately 3,000 witnessed a truncated performance. "It was pretty strange because we were using rental gear, which we really never did. That's the only time in Rainbow I can ever remember us not using our own stuff," Rondinelli explained.

Don Airey recalled, "After two numbers Ritchie walked off and took the rest of the band with him. Pointing to me to hold the fort while he got his amp fixed. So I did a solo and there was nobody there, I couldn't see any of the band, any of the crew. Just me on stage and I played for twenty-five minutes. Every trick in the book, 'Hawaii Five-O', 'Hawaiian Love Chant', Little Richard stuff trying to keep it going, desperately looking round. Eventually I thought the show's over and I walked off. I went back to the hotel and they were all sitting at the bar looking pretty pleased with themselves and I said to Colin 'get me out of here' and I got the first flight out in the morning and that was the last I saw of them."

Blackmore told *Circus*; "I'm not so crazy that I'd change a member of the group to make it worse. Don didn't see the point that certain people were becoming passengers who rested on their laurels, and that they'd rather be racing drivers." (*Circus* claimed that "it was a poorly concealed fact that Cozy Powell declared himself "unavailable" during some of the *Down To Earth* sessions so he could zip around the Continent in his Ferrari.").

Don Airey was quoted in the same feature; "I felt I'd done everything that I could with Rainbow. I blame myself for not doing more to keep Cozy in the band. The line-up we had at the time of *Down To Earth* had a hard, English style. I think we could have been another Led Zeppelin if we'd stayed together."

Blackmore said; "Don was Cozy's best friend. He didn't know that I had got Bobby Rondinelli to replace Cozy, and when he found out, he was fuming. I know Don's a good keyboard player; he's a musician's musician. But Don and I never spoke. It was a very tense situation. I can't blame him for taking that position about Rainbow; Don's not used to temperamental people like me. But it got to the point where I wanted Don out of the band."

Blackmore told *Kerrang!*; "It would be very easy for me to slag off everybody that's been in the band but it's a form of discipline not to. I do slag them off to only best friends but I try not to the press. Besides, there's never anything personal involved when I change personnel. If I had someone in the band who was a brilliant player I'd go 'anything you want, name it', of course I'd be Mr nice guy. But as soon as someone doesn't deliver the goods I go 'look you're not doing it right, what are you going to do?' and if they become snotty I go 'hey, on your bike, that's it', and it's always better for that person's career to say that he's left."

"It's not that I'm seeking perfection," the guitarist told *Circus* in May 1982. "I'm just looking for an affinity in the musicians I hire toward the way I feel about certain things... Nobody's ever left this group without being asked to leave. If I really wanted someone to stay in the band, I'd keep a rapport with that person and say, 'We can work this out.' Those people who've left — there's always been a reason."

To say that the line-up featured on *Difficult To Cure* didn't sound good together would arguably be something of an oversight though. The Virginia *Daily Press* reported in February 1981; "Heavy metal rock stars, it seems, never go away. They just keep regrouping their bands. The Tidewater area has seen this principle in action several times in the past few months. John Kay passed through with his revamped Steppenwolf. Kim Simmonds dropped by with yet another version of Savoy Brown, and this past weekend, Ritchie Blackmore and the latest incarnation of Rainbow hit the Peppermint Beach Club. All these bands are riding the crest of a renewed interest in heavy metal music, and Blackmore is certainly one of the founding fathers of the genre. An original member of Deep Purple, one of the world's most well-known heavy metal bands, Blackmore left that group in 1975 to form Rainbow. Although the band has had at least six different line-ups in as many years. Blackmore's fierce guitar work and his exacting choice of musicians have kept Rainbow near the top of the heavy metal heap. Rainbow's current configuration is an interesting reflection of Blackmore's temperament. Bassist Roger Glover, also the group's producer, was kicked out of

Deep Purple in 1973 at Blackmore's request. Blackmore picked up new drummer Bob Rondinelli off the Long Island club circuit, and new vocalist Joe Lynn Turner comes from a similar background. Keyboard player Don Airey comes from stints with Colosseum II and Cozy Powell's Hammer; Powell was Rainbow's drummer before Rondinelli took over."

"Deep Purple has been called the loudest band in rock 'n' roll history. If Rainbow hasn't taken over that title yet, it is certainly working on it. The band's set at the Peppermint Beach Club was ear-splitting, roof-shaking loud and that was before the sound was turned up. The capacity crowd didn't seem to mind the volume a bit, though. Rainbow has a hardcore following in this area, and the fans who turned out for the show were ready to rock and roll. And rock and roll they did, from the opening strains of 'Spotlight Kid' to the encore of 'Long Live Rock 'n' Roll'. Rainbow's energy level never tapered off, despite the hardest-driving stage in some time. Rainbow's sound is searing heavy metal, surprisingly fused with some almost classical keyboard elements. The group is given to extended solos during its songs, some of which last up to ten minutes. But while many groups turn their lengthy solos into excessive indulgence, Rainbow's remain interesting. The group played two cuts from its new album, 'Spotlight Kid' and 'I Surrender', tunes characterised by Blackmore's frenetic guitar work. There were songs to highlight each member's abilities: Airey's keyboard work on 'Catch The Rainbow', Glover's bass on 'Love's No Friend', and drummer Rondinelli's high-powered beat on 'Can't Happen Here'. Rainbow has a little fun with its music too, pulling in chords from 'Yankee Doodle Dandy' and Beethoven's Ninth. With an encore of 'Long Live Rock 'n' Roll' Rainbow left many in the audience convinced that rock really will live forever."

Why Straight Between The Eyes?

When word had done the rounds about Airey's departure from the band, Rainbow's management, Thames Talent, were inundated with audition tapes from hopeful candidates. The one that stood out was from one Berklee School of Music alumnus, David Rosenthal.

Rosenthal wasn't the only one invited to audition for the job though. Auditions were held at New York's Apple And Eve's nightclub on Route 110 Huntingdon Station. Even though local musicians were invited, the location was kept secret. One of those who auditioned there was Paul Morris who would later be invited to play on Rainbow's 1995 album, *Stranger In Us All* (for which he co-wrote the track, 'Black Masquerade').

Blackmore told *Kerrang!* about Rosenthal's audition; "I had a lot of people come to the auditions, and while most of them had the rock 'n' roll thing off they couldn't play any classical orientated piece on their own. However, I was given this tape by a friend, it was a piece by Liszt performed at a recital at the Boston University of Music. I said this guy is far too good for us, he'll probably be a musical snob, but after I'd auditioned everybody I could find, I invited him down and he played in such a brilliant way that I asked him to join. He didn't care that he wasn't taking a solo or doing an intro, he was so sick of playing Liszt and Bach that he was just happy to be part of a rock 'n' roll song."

Rainbow's tour manager Colin Hart said of the winning candidate; "His tape certainly impressed, even to the point of Ritchie saying he was almost too good, such was his classical background. However, we brought him to a rehearsal and after quite a few hours of jamming he was offered the job. David was only twenty-one years old and looked it. It was quite sobering to think that we three — Roger, Ritchie and myself were thirteen years older and way more experienced in this business. David would have to have a "handle with care" sign on him at least for the first few months (okay, weeks!)."

Kerrang! said of David Rosenthal: "One of a rare breed, and still only twenty one, he's a musician with a thorough grounding in the classics who still retains the ability to emote rock 'n' roll."

Turner told *Circus*; "The band's seemed more cohesive ever since Dave joined. Of course, nobody can expect to be with Rainbow forever and ever, including me. But I'm going to give it all I can for now. The attitude that no one will last hurt Don. He thought Ritchie was breaking up the band; that he was grasping at straws, not knowing what he was doing."

Glover told *The Palm Beach Post*; "Ritchie is a very good leader. He works very hard and expects others to do the same. He pushes himself to the limit, and he's always looking for players who give him what he wants. Making music is a constant series of dissatisfactions, which is all right as long as it's balanced with satisfactions."

Regarding the line-up changes that Rainbow had gone through up to that point, Glover said in July 1982; "I initially viewed the changes with distaste. But change does have its good points. If the band changes, it isn't allowed to stagnate. If you stay together too long the whole thing becomes very predictable."

With Rosenthal on board, it was time to get to work on songs for what would become *Straight Between The Eyes*.

Chapter Two

The Making of
Straight Between The Eyes

With *Straight Between The Eyes*, Turner would no longer have to sing in a key that was better suited to another singer's vocal range and style. It allowed him to contribute his own lyrics, many of which were based on his own experiences — something that had been apparent on the track, 'Jealous Lover' (it was originally used as the B-side for the 'Can't Happen Here' single but was given more radio play in the US than the A-side on the basis that the latter was considered too political).

It was considered in *Kerrang!* in 1982; "Not surprisingly, there are no chopped rhythms on the current LP, which both Blackmore and Glover agree was remarkably easy to record. Having examined a few songs by Russ Ballard and Brian Moran (of 'Magic' fame) and found none of them suitable, the band simply went ahead with their own ideas and had most of the work done in five weeks. A far cry from the recording of *Down To Earth*, an album put together by what many still regard as the definitive Rainbow line-up. Ritchie disagrees."

To which the guitarist explained; "I think anyone who says that was the best line-up must have been in the band then and isn't in the band now. Personally, I don't particularly like *Down To Earth*. *Difficult To Cure* and this one are my favourites. I like 'All Night Long', that particular track, and 'Since You Been Gone' as well, but there are tracks on there that were done under strained conditions to say the least. I liked the environment we were doing it in, a French castle, but the actual personnel were really grating on each other's nerves. What I liked about this new album was that I could come up with a couple of chords that I thought were valid and Joe would come out with a whole tune and brilliant words. He's a great lyricist as well as a great singer. It was so easy compared to what I was used to which was like pulling teeth. Ronnie (Dio) was good at producing lyrics and coming up with tunes, I could give him a vague melody and he'd know what I wanted, but after he left things went a bit sour. Roger had to write all the lyrics and I'd have to come up with an exact tune, there was no giving on the part of the singer whereas with Joe it's like a breath of fresh air."

Straight Between The Eyes, was recorded at Le Studio in Montreal, Canada. The studio had already been used by a range of diverse but big names such as Wilson Pickett, The Police and local boys Rush. Roger Glover was responsible for production with Nick Blagona on engineering. On his approach to producing, Glover told *Kerrang!*: "We might make some kind of compromise. It really depends on the situation. The thing is, every producer has his own style. There are some that completely dominate and don't let the group have any say whatsoever and others who let the band do exactly what they want. I fall somewhere between the two. I listen to everyone but, basically, I have the final say… On the last couple of albums, it's shown itself in my concern not to mix the bass too high. You tend to push yourself back so you don't get accused of hogging the limelight because you're at the controls. This new album is the first where I've asked for the advice of the engineer on the bass level."

The stability of the line-up for *Straight Between The Eyes* made the whole project more cohesive — not just generally but from a producing perspective. Glover told *The Palm Beach Post* in July 1982; "I produced the last three albums for Rainbow and the first two started before we got a vocalist, which is kind of like working in the dark. Everybody was in on the last album from the beginning. It was a big turning point and it shows in the music. The music sounds much more natural."

He told the *Detroit Free Press*; "This was certainly the easiest Rainbow album I've produced. It marked the first time we've gone into the studio with musicians who felt comfortable with each other. The problem with *Difficult To Cure* was that Joe joined the band as we were going into the studio, and he didn't have much time to contribute to the songs. But he has contributed to all the songs on this album, and he writes with the strengths and limitations of his voice in mind. The band's feeling at ease gave me a lot more to work with in the studio."

Happy days all round for Glover. He told *The Pittsburgh Press*; "In Rainbow, I'm fulfilling all three of my previous aims: playing, writing and producing."

Prior to recording what would become *Straight Between The Eyes*, Rainbow spent the cold final months of 1981 rehearsing in a house in Vermont, New England. Colin Hart recalled; "Come November, we journeyed up to Vermont to rehearse in a rented house for the album *Straight Between the Eyes*. It went well with "Little Joe" demonstrating once more that he was more than a foil for Ritchie, interpreting his riffs and music structure with strong lyrics. Joe's voice was exceptionally adaptable and he kept himself in shape too, so he was always "on the money" at rehearsals and recording, which matched perfectly Ritchie's ideals of professionalism and dedication. The Judy Garland tag didn't get mentioned anymore, so Joe had got his spurs. It was a good time to be

Rainbow - *Straight Between The Eyes*: In-depth

around them… Rehearsals done we moved on to a snowbound Montreal, Canada to Le Studio to start the album. The studio had been recommended to Roger by Nazareth, who he was producing. It was very picturesque overlooking a large frozen lake and we were up to our "small bits" in two to three feet of snow."

The working rapport between everyone was strong and committed. As Hart put it, "The actual recording of the album took only five weeks thanks to the rehearsal time in Vermont. The atmosphere was good and for Ritchie it was prank-heaven, a sure indication that all was well with him."

Just as well considering the cost of studio time. A letter to manager Bruce Payne at Thames Talent dated 26th October 1981 stated; "The following dates are held on your behalf for RAINBOW recording session: From Sunday November 15th until Sunday December 20th, 1981." The total cost was $72,000 US dollars but it did include accommodation, a housekeeper, groceries, catering and use of the telephone.

'The band certainly made the most of their time there. It was advocated in *Circus*; "Ritchie, Roger Glover, Joe Lynn Turner, drummer Bobby Rondinelli and organist David Rosenthal put six weeks' recording and ten days' digital mixing into the Polydor Records project. The care they took gives *Straight Between The Eyes* a cleaner sound than that of any previous Rainbow album."

Cooky Crawford — Blackmore's guitar technician at the time — recalled, "Le Studio was checked out by Colin back in September '81 and was confirmed to have the best and latest facilities available from engineers to caterers to absolutely beautiful landscape in the Laurentian Mountains of Quebec. The studio had a great reputation and boasted a pedigree line-up that included April Wine, Cat Stevens, Bryan Adams, Rush, The Police... and many many more."

"The Police had just recorded parts of *Ghost In The Machine* there just before we arrived. For Ritchie to be in a place that we couldn't play football at for more than a month just shows how determined and productive he could be."

'Death Alley Driver' is a strong opening track. Turner said in later years; "That song was about drug runs one and nine. Springsteen wrote about highway nine. That highway goes all the way through from the pier to New York. That song, I wrote about going on a drug run on highway nine. I was with a friend, who I found out I really didn't know that well. I ended up in this place where there were all these machine guns. This guy was a doctor that was brought in to analyse the cocaine that was coming in from Columbia. There were pounds of it. I stood there and I was thinking, 'What did you get me into to?' He was all coked out and I was like, 'Get me outta here.' I was sweating bullets. I wrote the song about that. Highway nine is a crap highway. It is a two-lane highway about as wide as an alley but it was the run where you went to get the Columbian blow, which was the best blow around."

'Death Alley Driver' is fun, memorable and incredibly melodic, as is the case where Blackmore quotes Bach's Toccata partway though the song (amusingly, on the video, this part coincides with footage of the band playing in a graveyard). It could be said that the duelling between Blackmore on guitar and Rosenthal on keyboards at this point in the song isn't too far removed from what Blackmore did with Jon Lord in Deep Purple.

Equally, the Bach reference indicates Blackmore's ongoing use of influence from classical music. The guitarist told *Sounds*; "That's what I try to do — use classical scales and progressions. My guitar parts are usually similar to classical violin parts — I don't copy them but I am influenced by them. I like listening to the scales they use. Having played for twenty-six years I don't get much enjoyment out of listening to rock 'n' roll anymore."

Upon being asked if Wagner's music would be an interesting point of influence for his music, Blackmore told *Sounds*; "No — he's too heavy. I'm more into the Baroque people and Händel. I like some of the renaissance music, and medieval music. I think a lot of sixteenth century music could be used in rock 'n' roll — it's very similar in many ways. Mostly I listen to organ recitals, especially in churches. They have a majestic quality that can root me to the spot, whereas with rock 'n' roll I often feel 'what's the point?' Church music makes me feel proud to be part of music. I tend to steer clear of rock 'n' roll and rock 'n' roll people in general, I find I've got nothing in common with them."

Whilst the rest of *Straight Between The Eyes* isn't as hard rock as 'Death Alley Driver', the song is an excellent introduction to where Rainbow were at after *Difficult To Cure*.

Cooky Crawford recalled what happened before Ritchie recorded his solo on the track; "Ritchie and I would walk to the studio through the woods and around a frozen lake to get the blood pumping and oxygen to the brain as he used to like to say. It was after one of these walks that Ritchie recorded that solo with the J.S. Bach influence. He always played these parts in the actual control room with a long lead stretching to his Aiwa and then leading out to the hardwood floor of the main studio where his Marshall Major head was. The cabinet was situated in a very reflective area on a hardwood floor and surrounded on two sides by the wall-sized windows."

"When Ritchie had the sound he envisioned it was this kind of inspired playing that was the result. It was super engineer Nick Blagona and his assistant Robbie Whelan who recommended where to place the cabinet and after a few trials in other areas was accepted by Ritchie and Roger. We had both Marshall and Bag End cabinets loaded with four Celestion G12-80 speakers which we used but I believe it was the Bag End cabinets we used for this one. These were very directional and you had to stand directly in front of them on stage to get the full effect so in the studio they were loud!"

"This was one of the few times I was present in the actual control room for a guitar solo as he liked total quiet and as few distractions as possible... so it was Ritchie, Roger as producer, and Nick Blagona and myself present at this time. I think Ritchie just wanted to show me how he did it as this was my first time in the studio with them. Most other times myself, Colin and Raymond would be outside in the lounge ready when summoned for help to fetch something needed or to move a cabinet or piece of equipment. It was an eye-opening experience being present for this great track."

Years later Turner said, "I co-wrote a few songs on *Difficult To Cure* but I didn't really blossom until *Straight Between The Eyes*. I think that is one of the band's signature albums. It was straight on. There were songs on that album like 'Power' and 'Bring On The Night' and 'Stone Cold' that were just great. We had some Blackmore-Turner songs but I also had some Glover-Turner songs. I think that album really showed them who I was. I was writing and singing and performing."

'Stone Cold' is more than an obligatory ballad. The inspiration for the song came from experience. The melody and lyrics go beyond the superficial ("Your words like ice fall on the ground, breaking the silence without a sound"). Although the sentimental character of the song seemed like new territory for Rainbow at that time, the track is still abundant in Blackmore's emotional guitar work.

Turner said of the inspiration for 'Stone Cold'; "We were out on the first tour and Roger had been left by his wife for a famous race car driver. He was very, very broken up over it. I looked in his room and I said, 'Rog, let's go to the bar.' He looked up at me and he had crying eyes. I said, 'What happened?' He just looked at me and said, 'She just stone cold up and left me.' I knew there was a song there. I ran back to my room and started writing the lyrics. It didn't come to fruition until we got the music. Ritchie would record a bunch of tracks and Roger and I would go through them and we would find the song and then we would teach it back to Ritchie. All Ritchie would do is jam on music and then we would take these pieces of music and make songs. We would then rehearse the song and work it all out. Later on, we were in the studio and it was totally a cold and snowy place. We were across from the studio and in between us was this little lake. Roger said, 'Let's go across the lake to the studio.' It was frozen over. We started walking across the lake. We didn't think anything of it because we had been playing hockey on it. All of the sudden we started hearing cracks. We looked at each other and we lay on our stomachs and sort of swam across the ice and snow until we got to the other side. We get to the studio and this front comes in and we are in this blizzard. I am singing 'Stone Cold' during this storm. I actually looked out of the studio as I was recording and looking at this blizzard and that is when I sang, 'Put me in the deep freeze'."

'Bring On the Night (Dream Chaser)' is not too different to a psychedelic seventies piece what with the use of warped effects against up-tempo hard rock. The urgency of the song comes as a welcome contrast to the pace of the previous track. Turner said of 'Bring On The Night (Dream Chaser)'; "Ritchie wrote the music and Roger had a part during the B section but the lyrics are all about me. It is all about trying to get into this business. All of those verses were about me."

Another hard rocker, 'Tite Squeeze' is blatant, melodic and energetic. Turner said of it; "Blackmore was making all of those great riffs. It is a great track. There was a lot of magic going on during those days."

To *Kerrang!*, Glover said of 'Tite Squeeze'; "It was a very natural song to do. Sometimes when you work in the studio and spend days on a track it ends up sounding a bit mechanical, whereas the tracks that sound fresh are the ones you accept, mistakes and all, because they happen to feel good and to me that's one of those tracks — and 'Stone Cold' is another. It could have been played better by all of us but it just felt good the way it was."

With an emotionally charged opening, 'Tearin' Out My Heart' is another song about the pains of love and deceit. It's delivered in a more upbeat way though. The chorus makes a strong impact in contrast to the softer verses. Overall, the structure of this song comes across as well thought out. Turner said of it; "Some people have told me that it is their favourite song on the album. I always give license to people's opinion. The song went over great in concert. The song had a lot of drama."

Some argued that the lyrics to 'Power' are rather banal but nevertheless, the song is catchy and memorable with highly rhythmic riffs. In terms of the audience that Rainbow wished to attract at the time, the song meets the objective.

Turner said of 'Power'; "We got ripped on that song because everyone said it was too commercial. That song was the concert favourite. Everyone was up off their seats and screaming 'Power'. I knew it would be that way when I wrote it. It is an autobiographical song. I was indulging myself."

Rosenthal shares a writing credit with Blackmore and

Turner on 'MISS Mistreated'. The song is enriched with Turner's powerful vocals and they complement Blackmore's guitar brilliantly. The starkness of Turner's delivery on the final words of the song makes them stand out in comparison to the rest of it. Like with 'Tearin' Out My Heart', 'MISS Mistreated' is structured in a way that bodes for lots of interesting contrasts.

In terms of how 'MISS Mistreated' was a titled so similarly to the Coverdale Deep Purple era song 'Mistreated', Turner said in later years; "That is why we did it. Ritchie was very into shoving things up other people's asses from afar. It didn't matter if it was Gillan or Coverdale or whoever. I remember telling him, 'I have this lyric called 'MISS Mistreated'.' He said, 'Well, we've already got one called 'Mistreated'.' I said, 'I know, but this one is 'MISS Mistreated'. It is more like who's mistreating who?' Ritchie loved it and he said, 'That is great. Let them suck on that for a while'."

So what was Blackmore's beef anyway? Well, according to Colin Hart, the guitarist had got into a fight with David Coverdale in 1980. It happened backstage at a Rainbow gig when Coverdale, against Blackmore's wishes, dropped by to say hello. The whys and wherefores aren't clear and it wouldn't be fair to speculate but endearingly, during the coronavirus pandemic, Blackmore and Coverdale did a musical collaboration over video call so one can only assume that things aren't as heated now.

As with 'Power', whilst some reviewers would go on to complain that 'Rock Fever' is too simplistic, the track does what it was designed to do in terms of how it translates well for live performance. It is up-tempo, repetitive hard rock full of hooks. The delivery is faultless on the album too though.

Turner said of 'Rock Fever'; "It was another concert favourite and it is another Blackmore/Turner song. Ritchie would write these riffs and I would take over and tell him, 'We've got to be more mainstream, Ritchie. We can't just keep writing about dragons.' We wrote about spiritual things like ghosts but we started writing about things that people on the street could relate to. It went over huge in concert. We were designing these songs for the live performance. It should have been a hit but in those days there was a lot of pay for play going on. There still is."

A seven-minute song, 'Eyes Of Fire' shows that Rainbow's commercial direction wasn't such that more complex tracks were put completely on the backburner. The track — on which Rondinelli shares a writing credit with Blackmore and Turner — recalls use of the same scale that Blackmore used in abundance on 'Gates Of Babylon' (the Phrygian scale — it has the effect of making a song sound otherworldly and mystical).

Against this though, Turner's vocals still manage to give the song a more mainstream flavour. A slight distortion on the vocals adds to the mysterious feel of the song. All of the instrumental parts sparkle and drive the song in a way that is forceful and effective. There are moments when the lyrics on 'Eyes Of Fire' almost hark back to Rainbow's earlier sound. For instance, "A demon, a daughter of madness, one look from her eyes could burn you alive...". This is an important track on *Straight Between The Eyes* in terms of how it shows that although Rainbow were certainly going for a different sound by this point, it wasn't always to the extent that Blackmore had moved *that far* away from the sound that so many fans had been drawn to back in the Dio era of the band.

The same could be said for the opening track on *Straight Between The Eyes* really. In that regard, the album goes full circle in terms of how, it is still distinctively typically Blackmore.

Rainbow - *Straight Between The Eyes*: In-depth

Turner said of 'Eyes Of Fire'; "I was in this very, very exclusive bar that was right across from the studio. I was across the bar from this very, very beautiful woman. I could see her looking at me in the mirror. In the mirror it really looked like her eyes were glowing. Okay, maybe I had a couple of beers but it was really weird. I ended up talking to her and she was a designer from Montreal. I have always wondered if she even knows she was the inspiration for that song."

Two singles were released from *Straight Between The Eyes*: 'Stone Cold' and (in Japan only) 'Death Alley Driver'. 'Stone Cold' got to number thirty-four in the UK and to number forty in the US. On the US Mainstream Rock chart though, it got to number one. It was also on the US Mainstream Rock chart that 'Power' got to number thirty-five despite not actually being released as a single. Mercury did issue a promotional 12" single for radio play and the song was a popular track on FM radio throughout the States.

It was considered in *Circus* in May 1982; "The inclusion of the cool, lyrical 'Stone Cold' in *Straight Between The Eyes* is proof that the formerly rough-edged Rainbow can turn out a stateside single as deftly as Foreigner can."

Videos were made just for 'Death Alley Driver' and 'Stone Cold'. In the 'Death Alley Driver' video, Turner plays on an arcade machine. It is actually Sega's *Turbo*.

Great as the video for 'Death Alley Driver' is, its run on MTV was cut short. Turner said in later years; "That video was on MTV. We were in that graveyard. We brought the drums and amps and everything to the graveyard. What got me was that one video, '18 And Life' (by Skid Row) and there were people shooting each other and our video got banned on MTV. Murder is okay but do not go into a graveyard! I think there really were a lot of dark forces chasing us around, I really do."

Also: "It was banned because we were in a graveyard promoting death... The lyrics went along with that when they said, 'Death is in the backseat of a big old black sedan' and there he was in the backseat with his top hat. Those were the days. Now videos are just soft porn."

Besides, the video was all done in good humour. It was considered in *Sounds* in December 1982; "In Rock Dream terms Blackmore would have to be painted as the murderous and gloomily glacial funeral director of Rainbow's 'Death Alley Driver' video, a Rachmanite rent collector with the conscience of a rabid rodent, or some madly morose monk twiddling thumbscrews in the torture chambers of the Spanish Inquisition. It is, he admits himself, an image he's worked hard to create and perpetuate. But it's actually as close to the real man as the *Sun* reporting is to the facts."

In the video for 'Death Alley Driver', it's amusing to see Blackmore sending up his mean and moody image by taking on the role of Death sitting in the back of a speeding car. The idea was Turner's. He told *Kerrang!*; "I do take credit for that. There's a line in the song 'he takes you on a corner with a wave of his hand, Death is in the back seat of a big old black sedan'. So I said to Bruce why don't we get Ritchie to play Death, why doesn't he sit in the back, and nobody went 'right, good idea' but the next thing I know Ritchie's coming in with the makeup man and his face is all white. And the figure who sits next to him in the car wearing a skull mask is actually his wife Amy!"

Cooky Crawford recalled; "I do believe this is the only studio video that actually shows Ritchie playing the right parts to his solo and Bobby really kills in this tune with his playing and stick twirls that he does better than anyone. David's solo too is epic and amazing in its complexity and arrangement...

just a great tune and video and one of Ritchie's top tracks in my opinion!"

Kerrang! considered of the video; "Involving a stunt motorcyclist and a good deal of location shooting around Connecticut's English-looking hills, it's an ambitious project — a welcome change from the standard heavy rock video that tends to be of the lip-synched, pseudo-live variety. Of course a video, no matter how exciting, can't make a bad song good but Rainbow needn't worry on that score as with 'Death Alley Driver' (and it's true of the album as a whole) they've struck a vein rich in commercial promise that should allow them to gain a wider audience without compromise or loss of credibility."

Crawford confirmed; "The video for 'Death Alley Driver' was filmed in two locations, the first being done in a Queens, New York rehearsal studio and the more interesting one being in a cemetery and in the streets of Easton, Connecticut. In the studio we set up a mini version of our stage set with two Marshall stacks for Ritchie, some of the grey bass cabinets which were used by David and Roger and Bobby's brand new black Yamaha kit. He had two kits just made for him and the red one he used on stage."

"For the video Ritchie brought a guitar he didn't use much anymore and liked to keep fans guessing about. This one was a blond Fender Stratocaster similar to the one he used during the California Jam."

"The cemetery scenes were filmed on a cold day in the fog! It was very strange setting up the gear in a cemetery early in the morning in the cold! The fog was pretty thick when we set up and we only put a couple of keyboards and again Bobby's black Yamaha kit. The band just kicks ass in this tune and I wished they had pushed this as a single. I don't think the fans would've thought they were as commercial sounding

The Making of Straight Between The Eyes

as they did if the heavier stuff was more highlighted!"

In April 1982, *Straight Between The Eyes* was reviewed in *Kerrang!*; "Rainbow are without doubt heavy metal's greatest phenomenon, and dare I say it, enigma. Which other heavy band could undergo such an almighty shift in direction from the overblown and altogether monumental sound of *Rising* to the classy heavy pop of *Difficult To Cure* and still maintain the respect of every denimed punter? I'd wager on that number being low — very low. I too have found much pleasure in the varied styles which Ritchie has followed (bar the infinitely tedious *Down To Earth*) and upon being treated to an earful of the single 'Stone Cold' from *Straight Between The Eyes*, I knew the man in black had done it yet again. 'Stone Cold' is a tower of controlled emotion and power, so Foreignerish — so excellent. You might be rapidly reaching the verdict that *Straight Between The Eyes* is American made, and aimed, yet this isn't by any means the whole case, for while the song structures of numbers such as 'Power' (in which Joe Lynn Turner excels, running in line with Foreigner's Lou Gramm all the way) and 'MISS Mistreated' are melody rather than riff based. Blackmore's playing and the spacious keyboards of new recruit David Rosenthal are so steeped in Rainbow's traditional sound that the UK sound is still apparent."

"All in all, this makes for an extremely interesting and satisfying conglomeration of diverse influential drawing points, which might easily have seen Rainbow falling on their backsides between two musical stools, but in fact sees the band grabbing the best of both worlds on an album which will certainly produce their biggest worldwide sales figures to date. *Straight Between The Eyes* will crack the American market wide open for Rainbow. Grudges are few, and far between but it is interesting to note that the band's favourite number, 'Tite Squeeze', also happens to be the one track which goes nowhere, and does nothing. I am actually trying to find something to knock to keep my critical faculties in order, and the truth of the matter is that of the Purple offshoot bands Rainbow are definitely the most exciting, innovative and simply the best."

To say that *Down To Earth* is "infinitely tedious" seems a bit harsh in the grand scheme of things but at the time the above review was written, there was no getting past the fact that some considered Rainbow's more recent albums to be preferable. For many fans, perhaps they had moved on from the fact that Rainbow had changed after the Dio albums and that after *Down To Earth*, each following album was made with a strong vision as to who the band's audience were.

Straight Between The Eyes was reviewed in *Record Mirror* in the same month; "At last Rainbow have cut their smooth approach and produced something with a bit more bite! It seems their personnel changes have given them a more direct, hard-hitting style although it's still aimed at the US market. *Straight Between The Eyes* will satisfy the most hardened headbangers among you and yet still remain highly accessible to the pop plebs. All the tracks on the album are written by group members Blackmore, Glover and newcomer Joe Turner — the man who replaced Graham Bonnet on vocals and that's another bonus!"

"The other new face, Bobby Rondinelli, although lacking the technical expertise of his predecessor Cozy Powell, is dynamically direct in his approach. I wasn't sure that he could fill Cozy's boots, but he has definitely come up with the goods. His performance on 'Eyes Of Fire', a track that contrasts sharply with the rest of the album, is superb. He picks up on the Asian influence and, careful not to drown the sitar player (Blackmore perhaps?), comes out with rhythms that are "Far East". But back to the good old boys.

The Making of Straight Between The Eyes

You can't forget the all-important screeching inventiveness of Blackmore's guitar wrenching. Even the near-ballad on the album, 'Tearin' Out My Heart', doesn't escape his multi-noted sheets of sound."

"Produced by Rainbow's Roger Glover, *Straight Between The Eyes* has all the hallmarks of an album that will yield a crop of successful singles. The one most likely to blast into the charts is 'Death Alley Driver', the opening track on side one. It immediately sets the ear drums vibrating. The fast and fluid sound — with Turner not so far off being a Bonnet clone — really drives the message home. With this blend of hard and fast heavy metal, 'Power' (which more or less explains itself) can be seen as an example of Rainbow relying on the music most of them must have played when they bought their first instruments. With all this in mind, the remaining tracks are typical Rainbow compositions with strong lyrics, and although the edges have deliberately not been smoothed this time, every number is tight and full of immediate, violent impact. Raw energy however, can be really appealing, and I wouldn't mind betting that this offering from the old reliables is going to be a winner. It's available in a fortnight's time. Enough said."

It was reviewed in *Sounds*; "Egomania. Or merely dedication to the perfection of the serpent's egg, the Ritchie Blackmore debate will no doubt continue a while yet. Whatever the final verdict, there can be no disputing that the current Rainbow line-up is as potent as any yet seen. Indeed, what king Dick appears to gunning his spit 'n' polished alchemy machine towards is a platinum-happy median mix of the poppy Graham Bonnet-era style, Americano rampage-rock hooks and just a pinch (no more, mind) of those garish instrumental pyrotech burns which he himself innovated, mastered (with Purple and after) and ditched a few yonkos

Rainbow - *Straight Between The Eyes*: In-depth

back. Those still interested in that redundant Popular Mechanics bilge should check out any Iron Maiden album."

"The first side boasts five variable slabs of attacking stink of the type calculated to upset serious rock writers with hardening circulation figures everywhere, via: 'Death Alley Driver', not much of a tune but a nifty all-out whine amalgam of Brit/USA hard rock matrixes, leaning heavily to the former with a stock footage guitar et keyboard dark head prowess-strut duel and subscribing to the big band theory at the close."

"Then 'Stone Cold' is icy, pre-masticated ersatz soul straight from the Foreigner mould, pomp-chord organ giving way to a short, itchy Ritchie soul-o. Follow that with 'Bring On The Night (Dream Chaser)', a halfway catchy shuffle ordinaire which might serve as a future forty five on a rainy day, the mediocre Free-funque of 'Tite Squeeze' and a fair tortuous trek over the slow motion metallic wastelands of grunt 'n' groan balladry, called 'Tearin' Out My Heart', and you've got an uncommitted cynic (me) withholding his vote until something mean shows up."

"And, praise the Lord, up it doth show at the very outset of the flippo, in the bone-crunching but candy coated shape of the magnificently shaking opus entitled 'Power'. Never has a title so concisely conveyed the essence of the bumph at hand. Starting with just ye olde axe and naught else, 'Power' boasts one of those riffs, like 'Louie, Louie' or 'Sweet Jane', which has a decidedly inevitable feel to it, an unstoppable happy hump-along sassiness which screams H-I-T from every note. It builds and bubbles and falls way too short for everyone's good, which is always a neat sign. Undoubtedly the best thing here."

"'MISS Mistreated' is, sadly, the other side of the coin, pure filler drag with vocalist Joe Lynn Turner back on the

The Making of Straight Between The Eyes

Lou Gramm trail again, but fluffing the pose somewhat badly. But I suppose the diehard brain haemorrhage mob have been waiting all through the blight for something like 'Rock Fever', a frantically indulgent piece of mesmerism short on tune but long on fret farce, where Blackmore wields his instrument like a Cobra charmer in India uses his flute. It's not the sound, it's the implication of the Strat, snakes being deaf and all. Ultimately music sans fangs, despite Roger Glover's vivid open-heart production."

"What the discerning fan ought to be delighting in (says I with confidence) is the experiment with lush, Arabian borrowed textures in 'Eyes Of Fire', a lengthy campfire dance with swirling string effects and haunting high-register guitar bleeps by Blackmore, all sheik, rattle and roll. Maybe Ritchie heard Bowie's 'Secret Life Of Arabia' or (more possibly?) Nico's similar 'Drama Of Exile', both of which tread the same sands. Metal goes moody and all of Rainbow acquit themselves beautifully. Hey! Is this "progressive"? Naw. But it's a million flashbombs from the duff Rainbow of several years ago and a quantum leap towards what any great rock 'n' roll should be about."

It was reviewed in *Muziekkrant Oor Holland*; "Let's face it: hard rock is an inward-looking genre. When I get a visit from a hard rock fan, it's like meeting a human from another planet. Yet it is and remains a type of music that can appeal to a large audience. How do hard rock acts like Foreigner, Van Halen and Joan Jett And The Blacks reach John Doe? By shamelessly recycling or using a slick ballad. But there is another way, with which also the more serious pop fan can be reached. Namely, by distinguishing yourself from the average hard rock mob, apart from flashy guitar work, by a well-considered use of keys, more experienced vocals and better compositions. Rainbow follows that road. The hell of

Rainbow - *Straight Between The Eyes*: In-depth

personnel mutations the formation has gone through — on *Straight Between The Eyes* Don Airey has been replaced by David Rosenthal — explains the lack of commercial success such as the above groups currently enjoy."

"The Roger Glover-produced album was recorded at Le Studio in Morin Heights, Canada, while the songs were digitally mixed and mastered. A recording process that 99% of the hard rock groups would not dare venture into, because if there is one recording process where nobodies fall through, then it is the digital one. Rainbow can take it, because their hard rock is, besides dynamic, extremely transparent and quite intelligent, while the group consists of nothing but "cracks". Ex-Fandango member Joe Lynn Turner is a fantastic lead singer, who can convey everything he sings about and credibly to the listener, Ritchie Blackmore's qualities as a guitarist are beyond question, while David Rosenthal often brightens up the instrumental framework with his keyboard contributions. The LP contains — with the exception of the absolutely commercial track 'Stone Cold' — not much American-oriented melodic hard rock. On the rest of the record, Rainbow keeps the sound English, creating a whole variety that is adept of the hard rock genre. For other fans, a healthy mix of hard rock and roll music will appeal and hit you "straight between the ears"."

And in *Hit Krant*; "Rainbow: what a band! Five exceptionally talented musicians, who put their individual qualities at the service of the group and not the other way around. That is the great strength of Rainbow: the total sound! Once again the quintet proves that they occupy a unique, very prominent place in the hard rock world. Their newest album *Straight Between The Eyes* again testifies top class. Melodic hard rock with excellent lyrics. The songs are played heavily but contain (luckily) no long solos. A fascinating LP, played by pedigree musicians who understand their trade. Listen and check out Joe Lynn Turner's voice on the single 'Stone Cold'."

And in *Cash Box*; "Deep Purple alums Ritchie Blackmore and Roger Glover continue their wild metallic antics on this no-holds-barred collection of raucous tunes dealing with fast cars, fast women and fast music. Having developed a faithful cult of fans since the inception of Rainbow back in the summer of 1975, Blackmore and co. may yet achieve superstar status with their newest offering, which at times recalls the best of Foreigner. AOR will flip for the one hundred miles per hour cut, 'Death Alley Driver' while cuts like 'MISS Mistreated' should appeal to the cynical lover in every brainbasher."

The *Reading Evening Post* reviewed it in May 1982; "Rainbow are back after yet more line-up changes. Ritchie Blackmore's band is the one which sticks closest to the original Deep Purple sound. Gillan and Whitesnake have moved on but Blackmore's speed-freak guitar and the presence of bassist Roger Glover brings back memories of *Machine Head*. *Straight Between The Eyes* has quieter tracks, like 'Stone Cold' though. It's altogether one of the best things Rainbow have yet done."

As did *Cleveland Scene*; "Ritchie Blackmore has never really cared what people think of his music. Fortunately, many of the songs Ritchie penned during his days with Deep Purple and most recently, Rainbow, were well-received but Rainbow's last release, *Difficult To Cure*, definitely was not up to par compared to previous Rainbow LPs. As a follow up to that last album, *Straight Between The Eyes* is a fresh, vibrant effort. 'Death Alley Driver' kicks off the LP in fine style with Blackmore's guitar sounding much the same as it did on 'Highway Star' years ago, while the more relaxed sounds of 'Stone Cold' add a melodic touch to the album.

Rainbow - *Straight Between The Eyes*: In-depth

The most dominant song on *Straight Between The Eyes* is 'Power'. This irresistible tune features one of the most catchy chord arrangements Blackmore has come up with in years. It has that unique quality that makes you want to hear it again and again. *Straight Between The Eyes* is a real winner. Even if you're not a Ritchie Blackmore fan, *Straight Between The Eyes* is sure to please."

Stargazer fanzine editor Simon Robinson wrote; "From the sublime to, well I haven't actually bothered to get it yet. Lack of funds is the excuse, but the days when Ritchie's latest offerings were an essential buy ended with *Long Live Rock 'n' Roll* as far as I'm concerned. The radio preview only confirmed my fears, I couldn't see much difference between the Rainbow track and the two which followed it — and they were by two different bands. Still, I'll get it some day."

Contributing to the same magazine, the late Mark Putterford said; "The album rockets off to a powerful and frantic start with 'Death Alley Driver', set firmly in the 'Highway Star' tradition including the final solo from Ritchie. 'Stone Cold' is next, a straight Foreigner rip-off but I like it and I think the press were too harsh on it, expecting Ritchie to be heavy all the time. 'Bring On The Night' is pleasant, and a possible catchy follow up forty five. In contrast, 'Tite Squeeze' is a plodding 'LA Connection' affair I could see Ronnie James Dio doing. 'Tearin' Out My Heart' again smacks of Foreigner, but has some fine singing from Turner especially at the end with his high scream on the guitar — great. Side two opens with a kind of AC/DC-type riff, but 'Power' develops into quite a good song (great headbanging stuff — yuk). 'MISS Mistreated' is straight out of the Whitesnake songbook, thumping bass, background keyboards etc., and is probably the worst track on the album despite Blackmore's soloing. 'Rock Fever' makes me cringe

The Making of Straight Between The Eyes

— lemme-see-ya-rock-lemme-see-ya-roll — god; makes me wonder if he hasn't run out of ideas altogether. The last track, 'Eyes Of Fire' is weird. At first it seems like a dreary endless noise, a bit like 'Gates Of Babylon' and an attempt to recreate the '77 era Rainbow. I haven't made up my mind if it's duff or a gem yet. So what have we got? A good album but hardly one which demands to be played over and over. The line-up is strong; Rondinelli is the best he's had since Paicey. Joe Lynn is superb, and the new guy fits in well, so why aren't they as good as they ought to be? I think the answer lies with Blackmore and Glover. I still don't like Roger's production or indeed his current poppy style of bass work and Blackmore just frustrates me with his insistence on sticking to the same style and sound, very sad when you think what he can and has done in the past. However even if I don't much like the direction, *Straight Between The Eyes* is the best they've made in a long while."

It was no secret that Rainbow were making a deliberate attempt to be more commercial. "Unquestionably, we've turned in a more accessible direction on the last few albums," Blackmore explained to *Asbury Park Press* in April 1982. "A few years ago I would have insisted that selling records means nothing. I realise now that a statement like that is made only by someone who isn't selling many records. I imagine that seeing a sickening band like the Bee Gees sell millions of records helped me form that philosophy. Every artist wants people to buy their product, and even though I'm certainly not happy with the more commercial aspects of rock and roll, I am happy that our albums are doing well."

The decision didn't come without criticism though. Turner told *Kerrang!*; "For some reason that seems to be a dirty word with everyone, but all the bands I know, Zeppelin included, they're commercial. Who're they kidding? Listen, we're tired of not reaching the American public, tired of not reaching people who like a decent song. If you can play it, do it! We were in some hellhole, Edmonton, Canada, I think, and I said to Bruce (Payne) our manager 'we can crack the commercial market and keep our integrity'. And he looked at me and went, 'have another drink'. But I said 'no, I swear it, we can' and I've started to see that happen on *Straight Between The Eyes*. We're getting into a bluesy feel and Ritchie's not so uptight about it all being smash headbanging stuff. I think he'll enjoy playing 'Stone Cold' on stage."

Chapter Three

Live Between The Eyes

The release of *Straight Between The Eyes* was supported with an extensive tour that would see Rainbow cover a lot of ground between May and November 1982. Not only did they perform in North America, Japan, and parts of Europe that the band had already engaged with as part of previous tours, but also new territories of Spain and Portugal.

Not having been too pleased with Rainbow's tour in 1981, by 1982, there was everything for Blackmore to play for. In April 1982 it was reported on in *Kerrang!* that "on the next British tour the band will invoke the spirit of their stage-spanning rainbow by returning to an elaborate stage production (giant mechanical eyes that presumably swivel and illuminate would seem to be one idea), a marked contrast to the sparse use of effects on the last UK dates While Ritchie feels that keeping things simple was the right decision, a reflection of the poor economic climate and the resultant no-frills mentality of the audience, he wasn't overly pleased with the tour as a whole."

Overall, the Straight Between The Eyes tour had been scheduled with the American market in mind. It was on the American leg of the tour that Rainbow were in the main supported by Iron Maiden and 38 Special. Colin Hart recalled; "Bruce and the agency were planning the next attack on the US market with the release of *Straight Between The Eyes* and the inevitable tour to promote it. Rainbow were now very

Rainbow - *Straight Between The Eyes*: In-depth

mainstream rock, but for all that, still considered *the* band to support to get on the rickety ladder to rock stardom."

Hart recalled; "Ritchie decided we would travel by tour bus rather than flying, which made life a lot easier for me as we were not constricted by airline timetables or the fuss of checking in to airports. Travelling was now far more flexible."

The tour also saw Rainbow perform at some of the smaller and all-too-often overlooked venues. Compared to some of the tours that Hart had been on with Deep Purple, the Straight Between The Eyes tour was smooth in terms of its geographical planning. In particular, in the late sixties, a number of Deep Purple's tours had involved a sequence of gigs that were geographically far apart from each other from one day to the next.

Not everything about the Straight Between The Eyes tour was perfect though. Rainbow didn't perform in the UK as part of this tour. The reasons behind it were never stated explicitly but the decision is an understandable one perhaps in terms of how the record was very much geared towards the American market. Considering the time and energy it takes to tour, why do dates in places where the scope to sell records might be less lucrative? A difficult one to weigh up perhaps, but still.

Kerrang! made this point in April 1982: "What British fans will make of the album remains to be seen, though the fact that Rainbow have no plans to play here before April '83 may sour the judgment of a few. In America, however, a strengthening of their position looks certain. Already the band can draw crowds of 20,000 in major cities like Los Angeles and Chicago but it's in the smaller towns on the circuit that they daren't venture out of the 3,000 seaters. In this respect, *Straight Between The Eyes* may help them move up a notch though to label it a dollar-hungry compromise would be wide of the mark."

It could be said that Blackmore wasn't too keen to perform in the UK around this time anyway. *Kerrang!* asserted; "The music press, who've given Rainbow a bit of a hard time of late, are essentially London based. Even onstage Ritchie's aware of their presence." To which the guitarist was quoted; "I can mentally see them writing their little reviews going 'oh this is fucking awful, it's so boring', and I can't concentrate on what I'm playing. Yet the kid in the front row is saying 'come on, yeah' and I feel obligated to him, but the next second I'm back into the mental picture of the review which I shouldn't be. But then most musicians have taken up an instrument because they're sensitive, I know I did when I was eleven. I took up the guitar because I was moody, highly strung and wanted attention, so I suppose that when you come in for bad reviews it hits you. I certainly live with it, it stays there. The problem with Rainbow, though, is having so many ex-members. These ex-members have journalist friends so, without mentioning names, it can't be helped that we have a lot of enemies in the press."

Glover told *Kerrang!*; "American music really brings me down, though we're moving in much the same direction. On a personal level I don't know if I'm too happy about that. I'm happy if the band's successful doing it, but I can understand people's criticism of Rainbow going American, as it were."

By the time it came to the Straight Between The Eyes tour, Turner had attuned his stage presence to what the other members of Rainbow expected from him. He told *Goldmine* in 2008; "I was overzealous, and I was overdoing everything. Ritchie and Roger helped to grow me up. Ritchie would say, 'Just wrap your fucking legs around the mic stand and sing with all that soul power that you have. Quit prancing around the stage like some sort of poofta'. It made sense, and I finally got it. Now I kind of combine a little of both because I am an American and not a stoic, pretentious Englishman."

The first date of the tour took place at the SIU Arena in Carbondale, Illinois. It was reviewed in student paper, *The Daily Egyptian* in May 1982; "Rainbow, led by former Deep Purple guitarist Ritchie Blackmore, put on a show Friday night that had many ups and a few downs — but generally it was one of the better rock concerts the Arena has had this year. Rainbow started the show with a recording of Judy Garland singing 'Somewhere Over The Rainbow'. As the song played, a backdrop with hypnotic eyes painted on it was unveiled. Then the band ignited the frenzy of the crowd of about 4,000 by firing up an enlivened performance. Sure enough, the audience's response said they knew they were not in Kansas anymore, as the line from *The Wizard Of Oz* goes. Audience members frenziedly waved arms resembling tree branches in a hurricane. Blackmore looked generally as if he were in the midst of melancholic lethargy, but did erupt into a few spurts of activity, like leaping in the air to land on his knees, furiously plucked his guitar. He performed very well."

"The Rainbow concert did not under-do the flashing lights, and they were not overdone either. Rather, they were balanced to accent the show, not to overpower it. Blackmore actually has the skill to play the guitar and not make the mindless noise that most rock guitarists pawn off as solos. His version of the fourth movement of Beethoven's Ninth displayed the skill of a classical guitarist. However, Blackmore botched a riff during his lacklustre rendition of the Deep Purple hit 'Smoke On The Water'. Old Rainbow tunes though, like 'Man On The Silver Mountain' and 'Long Live Rock 'n' Roll' were done well and fast."

"Blackmore was not alone in presenting a good mood.

Drummer Bobby Rondinelli performed a fine drum solo that did not become long and boring. However, keyboard player David Rosenthal's solos were a disappointment. Rosenthal pounded the keyboard with his fist and carried on in a way that came across more like a childish tantrum than serious music playing. His synthesiser playing during his tenure in the spotlight sounded like the *Pac-Man* game. Vocalist Joe Lynn Turner performed energetically and sounded a lot like Foreigner's Lou Gramm. But despite all his energy Turner lacked the magnetism of Blackmore, who played with an air of eerie melancholy, head hung low, his dark eyes occasionally sweeping across the stage and audience. The opening band, Charlie Midnight, also deserves mention. Arena Director Gary Drake said the band wanted to open for the concert very badly."

A performance that took place at the Civic Centre in Lansing, Michigan, 13th May was reviewed in the *Lansing State Journal*; "True rock fans are a special breed of beings. They can stand all night on wobbly chairs in a room stuffed tighter than a band-aide box filled with life rafts. Rock and rollers can cope with heat which could melt bumpers off of old Buicks. Most of all, true rockers love their music loud. Thursday night, in the Lansing Civic Centre, a sell-out crowd of such creatures were made happy. They stood on their feet as three bands performed almost four hours. Iron Maiden, 38 Special and Rainbow blew the blemishes off the faces of a mostly young audience with some speaker shakin' rock. Ritchie Blackmore led Rainbow through some thunderous music that kept the crowd wet with sweat. It was warm enough inside the Civic Centre to fry a sidewalk sunny side up. Rainbow was able to keep the temperature high with high volume music."

A performance that took place at Richfield Coliseum,

Rainbow - *Straight Between The Eyes*: In-depth

Ohio, was reviewed in *Cleveland Scene* in May 1982; "Rainbow's short, interrupted set was typical of the show rendered by Ritchie Blackmore and company in the past. Older Rainbow material was in short supply, consisting only of 'Long Live Rock 'n' Roll' and 'Man On The Silver Mountain'. Newer material from last year's *Difficult To Cure* album and the more recent *Straight Between The Eyes* LP was abundantly the remainder of the evening. Lead vocalist Joe Lynn Turner seemed to be straining at times, but really belted it out on the band's current single, 'Stone Cold'. His vocal delivery here and on 'MISS Mistreated' was really precise, down to each individual note."

"Ritchie Blackmore, along with Roger Glover on bass, Bob Rondinelli on drums, and newest member, Dave Rosenthal on keyboard, put forth a good instrumental effort. However, while Blackmore's guitar wizardry remains second to none, his unpredictable emotions and desire to have everything nothing less than perfect, can sometimes cause problems. A slight hum in the monitor system resulted in Ritchie walking off the stage, while roadies frantically tried to fix the problem which caused a ten-minute delay in the show. With everything under control, Rainbow returned finally breaking into a short, but potent version of 'Smoke On The Water'. This was a real treat that kept the restless audience pacified."

A performance that took place at the La Crosse Centre on 3rd June was reviewed in *The La Crosse Tribune*; "La Crosse is not exactly a hotbed of heavy metal enthusiasm. Country music fans filled the La Crosse Centre to overflowing twice on Wednesday for the Kenny Rogers concert. But it was a different story Thursday night. About 2,500 people attended the Rainbow-UFO-Riot concert. Riot, a New York based band, was the opening act and unless it does some tightening

Live Between The Eyes

up, it is doomed to remain an opening act... The double-billed main attractions of the evening were heavy metal bands UFO and Rainbow. UFO followed Riot and the difference was apparent from the first chords played. UFO kept the crowd up and screaming with 'Too Hot To Handle' and 'Lights Out'."

"But Rainbow is the band that stole the show. With the leadership of legendary guitarist Ritchie Blackmore, of Deep Purple fame, the band is deeply rooted in heavy metal. But Rainbow plays heavy metal with a twist, serving up some of its music with a classical flavour. Add to that a good light show, explosions and showers of fireworks and this is a band which will catch your attention. It grabbed the audience with 'MISS Mistreated', which sounds as if it was written specifically to be sung in front of an audience. The band is tight and cohesive and really got going when lead singer Joe Lynn Turner began singing 'Stone Cold', which is currently blazing its way up the charts. As Turner sang, two eyeballs painted on a black curtain at the back of the stage spewed forth beams of red light, darting out at the audience."

"The band delighted the audience by playing an old Deep Purple standard for the first encore 'Smoke On The Water'. The song was, of course, accompanied by clouds of smoke and the stage was appropriately drenched in a rainbow of colours. Rainbow chose a rather peculiar song to open its second encore — the Beatles' 'Yesterday'. Joe Lynn Turner certainly does not have the voice of either Paul McCartney or John Lennon, so he and the band would do well to forget the Beatles and stick with heavy metal. With three bands performing, and two encores by Rainbow, the concert stretched to four hours."

For the *Stargazer* fanzine, a fan wrote of Canada's London Gardens Arena gig of 7th June; "The Scorpions came on around 9pm and did a good show, then there was a

Rainbow - *Straight Between The Eyes*: In-depth

long intermission while roadies etc. changed sets. I must say there were a lot of Scorpions fans there but I think Rainbow did a better job. I scuttled off to the far right aisle for an excellent view of the stage. After the Garland intro, some drums and keyboards, the lights went on and they went into 'Death Alley Driver'. Turner looked like your typical heavy metal singer but Glover surprised me decked out in a white suit and hat, like a southern yankie gentleman. He looked rather silly! Blackmore (in black!) looked extremely bored during the first song, hung around the drums and didn't take his eyes off the floor, though he perked up during the next number and looked a little more with it. Behind the band was a canvas sheet with eyes painted on and lights flashing on it. In all honesty it looked pretty terrible. I can recall they also did 'Stone Cold' — very popular here, 'Long Live', and 'I Surrender'. They did nothing off the first album — a disappointment."

All tours are full of great gigs and bad ones and the Straight Between The Eyes tour was no exception. Things didn't go too well when Rainbow played at Milwaukee. Colin Hart said; "On June 5th, we played The Alpine Valley Music Theatre in Milwaukee and it was freezing despite being early summer. It was the wind, you see, which must have been from the north straight from the Arctic sweeping across the lake. Ritchie stood it for thirty minutes then did the old "guitar off/ lay on top of amp/switch off/exit stage left silently" routine and we were done much to the disgust of the locals who were obviously made of far hardier stuff."

In June 1982, under the headline of "Scorpions Win "Terrific" Rating; Headliner Rainbow No Match", *The Morning Call* reported; "At the Allentown Fairgrounds last night, there was ample proof that subtlety doesn't count for much in the vast venues of America. In other words, heavy metal bands once again had come to town. That meant big sounds, big concession sales, a big crowd, and a joyous, festive atmosphere that tapped its energy from Woodstock-era pop culture. Much of the estimated crowd of 6,500 arrived too late to hear New York band Riot, which had the distinction of opening up this, the first large-scale outdoor concert of the year... After the Scorpions left the stage, it became apparent that most of the crowd had come to see headline act Rainbow."

"Lit matches and high-pitched screams greeted guitarist Ritchie Blackmore and his ensemble while pseudo fog filled the stage and a tape of classical music blasted from a mountain of speakers. Despite the opening fanfare, Rainbow proved to be no match for the Scorpions. Blackmore showed he could still construct a neck-breaking riff or two, just like he did while playing with Deep Purple. But when considering that other rockers like Eddie Van Halen and Rush's Alex Lifeson are redefining the guitar-hero role, Blackmore's blues-based riffing and overly long soloing sounded hopelessly old hat. Enthused, one longhaired teen in an Iron Maiden Killer tour t-shirt: 'Man, these guys are great.' The older, wiser guy next to him rolled his eyes and asked: 'Where's Motörhead when you need 'em?'"

It's interesting to note how some journalists categorised Rainbow as a heavy metal band. In fact the term had become commonly applied to most rock music of the harder variety, especially in the States where the terminology was originally coined. It is a term that many fans would argue is not applicable to Rainbow in view of their overall discography. However, the fact that it was the early eighties and that Blackmore himself sought to appeal to American audiences who were into heavy metal makes it understandable.

On balance, the same performance was reviewed in the

Rainbow - *Straight Between The Eyes*: In-depth

Stargazer fanzine; "Rainbow did a smallish (twelve to fifteen thousand) outdoor festival at the Allentown Fairgrounds on June 15th, supported by the Scorpions plus Riot. They played well but not brilliantly; solos kept very short. Tracks were 'Spotlight Kid', 'MISS Mistreated', 'I Surrender', 'Can't Happen Here', 'Stone Cold', 'Tearin' Out My Heart', Beethoven's Ninth, 'All Night Long', 'Power', 'Long Live' and 'Smoke On The Water' for an encore with all guitars kept intact."

No guitar smashing at the end?! Perhaps like those who wrote the reviews, the man in black wasn't having the best time that day.

In July 1982, *Cash Box* reviewed the performance that had taken place at Madison Square Garden on 19th June. If older fans weren't happy with Rainbow's direction, the band's scope to perform at this 20,000 capacity venue was a definite indication of how much more successful they had become:

"PolyGram recording group Rainbow made its return to the Big Apple with a raucous, severe show meant only for the strong at heart and was never afraid to augment the effect of its music with violent stage effects. But, to add a dash of style to its particular alloy of heavy metal, the group often took advantage of the classical backgrounds of lead guitarist Ritchie Blackmore and keyboardist David Rosenthal. Prefacing the show with a prop shaped like bloodshot eyes that beamed directly into the audience, the group led off with the hard-driving 'MISS Mistreated', a noisy number that kept the predominantly teenage male crowd sufficiently roused to stay on its feet throughout."

"Keyboardist David Rosenthal led into the equally rowdy 'I Surrender' with a serene synthetic eighteenth century harpsichord solo. He also resorted to the sounds of a church organ to prelude 'Stone Cold' which, with the strong vocals of Joe Lynn Turner, brought home the pain of the song's character. Lead guitarist Blackmore showed his chops on 'Tearin' Out My Heart' and towards the end of the show, did a long guitar solo taken from his days with Deep Purple. Predictably, he encored with 'Smoke On The Water', the latter's 1972 hit, which was accompanied by formula fog effects."

This review claims that the show opened with 'MISS Mistreated' but it was actually 'Spotlight Kid'. For the first month of the tour 'Death Alley Driver' had been the opener but was then dropped from the set.

In June 1982, a fan wrote in *Stargazer* of a gig that took place at the Providence Civic Centre; "The Civic Centre was packed. Over 10,000 screaming white middle class kids with Riot and the Scorpions to warm them up. Finally the PA was blasting out Pomp And Circumstance, then the *Oz* intro. The lights came on and Rainbow ploughed into 'Spotlight Kid'. Amidst dry ice is a dapper looking Glover in white. A huge pair of (bloodshot) eyeballs — no kidding! — are lowered from the lighting rig and hover above the band, gazing left and right with lights shining out through the pupils. Hmmm."

"Solo is different, he did the 'Difficult To Cure' one for some reason. Exit huge eyes thankfully, they were pretty funny really. 'MISS Mistreated' and 'I Surrender' next, unexceptional. Band played well and the new keyboard guy fits in well. Turner then dedicated the next song to 'the British Navy' — you guessed it — 'Can't Happen Here'; fast version slowing down into a very nice quiet bit, before becoming 'Tearin' Out My Heart' which came together much better live with more feeling. The end was different too and Ritchie finished with a great rave-up solo."

"Up until then I felt he was just going through the motions.

Next; 'All Night Long', one I've never been fond of. The backdrop's eyes light up and Ritchie is using his old bass pedals, before they do a boring audience participation thing in the middle followed by a brief keyboard break featuring 'Child In Time' then into 'Stone Cold'. Out pop those eyes again for 'Power' which again is much improved live, with another excellent solo from Ritchie that really got the crowd going. The pace now slowed as Glover and the keyboard guy do some riffing together before keyboard solo time; actually quite imaginative and better than his predecessor. Drums next and, though I hate to admit it, really better than anything I'd seen by Cozy."

"I think Blackmore really has got a good band now; maybe room for Turner to improve but even he wasn't too bad! The band return to start up 'Long Live Rock 'n' Roll' which the crowd take up, as the stage goes very dark for some minutes. We wonder what's going on when it suddenly explodes with light, fireworks, sparklers etc., and the end of song. Band leaves, crowd go wild, encore! Blackmore is in complete control, frantic soloing to 'Kill The King', turns around hurls his guitar into his amp and it explodes! He then plays it with his feet, tiring of that he smashes the crap out of it and climbs the speaker stack to finish it off up top. He's soon back on the stage for a burst of 'Stargazer' and a short 'Smoke On The Water' — very rousing I might add! End of show. Well paced throughout, not the best Ritchie I've seen but one of the best shows overall since the Rising tour."

Another fan described their experience of the gig in the fanzine: "What inspired me to drive three hundred miles there I dunno, but the show was better than Allentown although the crowd was young and uneducated and Ritchie must have known he didn't have to try too hard to please them. Two huge swivelling eyes with spotlights that shone out of them onto the audience came down during the opener 'Spotlight Kid', and there was also a backdrop of the sleeve with eyes glowing during 'Stone Cold'. They used a fair number of fireworks up too, and Ritchie left out Beethoven. Ritchie attempted to bust his guitar but after the neck came off he couldn't dent the body. After the show I booked into a hotel nearby which turned out to be the one the band had chosen. I saw Ritchie later in the bar looking bored. I thought he'd fallen asleep at one point until I saw he was after a bowl of peanuts which he lined up on the edge of the table and proceeded to flick at passers by!"

Of the gig that took place at the Philadelphia Spectrum on 27th June, a fan wrote for *Stargazer*; "There was a wildly enthusiastic crowd, all familiar with Rainbow's work and it was the best show of them all. Ritchie responded by playing like a wild man — he was absolutely brilliant. They dropped 'I Surrender' (no loss) and reinstated 'Beethoven'. Ritchie and Bobby did a nice jam and then a surprise as they resurrected the blues bit off *On Stage*, only a hundred times better with lots more bluesy guitar from Ritchie. It was just one of those nights — he couldn't be stopped. Awesome. Come encore time he burst on amidst a flurry of notes and then began 'Jealous Lover'. They did the whole song and ripped into 'Smoke On The Water'. After that they returned again while Ritchie sacrificed another guitar, flinging the bits at his amp which burst into flames and sticking the rest into the cabinet. He brought on a replacement and proceeded to play this with the butt end of the broken one, it was the best destruction since Purple days."

Under the heading of "Rainbow's Concert Vanishes After Only Nine Numbers", the *Pittsburgh Press* reported on the following gig at the Stanley Theatre; "Bands do change their names. For instance, the Quarrymen became the Beatles, the High Numbers became The Who, the Golliwogs became Credence Clearwater Revival and Mother McCree's Uptown Jug Champions became the Grateful Dead."

"Rainbow, based on last night's date in the uncomfortably muggy Stanley Theatre, has a perfect substitute in the wings — "Ripoff". Nine songs — that's right, only nine, and no 'I Surrender' or 'Man On The Silver Mountain', two of their better-known ones — and one crummy, two-song medley encore in just seventy five minutes on stage. And what comprised the medley? One verse and the final chorus of 'Since You Been Gone', one of Pittsburgh's most popular songs, and two verses and choruses of Deep Purple's classic 'Smoke On The Water' (for the uninitiated, guitarist Ritchie Blackmore and bassist Roger Glover were Purple members). That's a rotten way to treat people who paid good money to hear, presumably, one of their favourite bands and certainly their favourite songs by that band. No wonder the booing was almost as deafening as the music had been when the stage went dark after 'Smoke'."

"A few slow guitar lines were heard and then the house lights came on — the fans thought they'd be getting more, and it was tape, not Blackmore. What they'd gotten to that point was exactly what Rhett Forrester, lead singer for the opening act, Riot, called his band's music: 'a heavy metal alternative'. There's no denying songs like 'Spotlight Kid', 'MISS Mistreated', 'All Night Long', 'Power' and 'Long Live Rock 'n' Roll' are hard and heavy, and there's also no denying Rainbow plays that style as well as anyone."

"Yet there were plenty of more musical touches: the slower, bluesy duet between Blackmore and singer Joe Lynn Turner on 'All Night Long'; David Rosenthal's "haunted castle" organ opening to the Foreigner-sounding 'Stone Cold', several highlights on the long 'Difficult To Cure'.

Live Between The Eyes

Those included Blackmore's making his electric guitar sound like an acoustic one, stick-tossing Bobby Rondinelli's drum solo on which he used his hands in lieu of sticks at one point and Rosenthal's keyboard solo, which ended with the *Looney Tunes* opening."

"Blackmore, of course, added most of the spice. He plays effortlessly, standing like a statue with only fingers moving (flying, actually) and an occasional wig-wag of his head. He comes to bodily life only after or before his part is over. There was plenty to see as well: dry ice fog, flash pots, scads of coloured lights, spotlights in a frame around a large gong behind Rondinelli and, to celebrate the holiday a few days early, five jets of sparklers at the edge of the stage and some firecrackers in the audience to boot."

"The most striking of all was a huge pair of bloodshot eyes with green irises (the quintet's current album is called *Straight Between The Eyes*) suspended on a truss and lowered over the band to beam searchlights over the crowd. This was a terrific visual effect. Riot couldn't compete with that, such is the lot of opening acts. So this quintet had to make do with its music, and just looking at the huge banks of speakers at stage left and stage right told you what was coming. Sort of. Just like Rainbow, Riot plays it hard and loud yet offers just enough seasoning here and there to avoid the "mindless" tag."

A positive review despite the complaint that Rainbow only played nine numbers. In such instance, it is worth noting that the press at the time were not averse to playing on what many perceived to be Blackmore's image. Glover told the *Detroit Free Press* in May 1982; "I think Ritchie's temper has been a bit distorted by the press. True, he is difficult at times, but he's certainly no monster. If he was as ill-tempered as some would have you think, I couldn't stand to be around him. Ritchie's a very quiet man. Though he's never come out and said he appreciates me, I'm sure he does. I think it's understood. And it isn't like I don't get anything from playing with him. He's a phenomenal musician and his taste in music is impeccable. I respect that."

Glover also told *Cleveland Scene* that month; "Ritchie's unpredictable. When he's good, he's out of this world. He's brilliant, but when he's bad, people call him "moody" and "weird". He's not really. He's a very straightforward guy — a very nice guy. He believes in what he believes. That's the strength of his success 'cos he believes so much in what he does. If something's gone wrong with the sound or in his head or with the audience he does things about it."

With the tour moving on with different support acts, Steve Gett reported on the 20th July show in *Melody Maker*; "At 7:30 the houselights go down in Washington's giant Capital Centre auditorium as those in attendance prepare to enjoy a feast of metal mayhem. And a fine evening's entertainment it promises to be too... First to hit the stage are those lovable letchers The Rods... Next on are Krokus... Finally, Rainbow hit the stage, kicking off with 'Spotlight Kid'. This is the first proper date on the second leg of their Straight Between The Eyes tour and what an absolute killer it turns out to be. The man in black is in brilliant form and plays some of the best lead breaks I've yet to witness him deliver in concert."

"Aside from the omission of the riotous 'Death Alley Driver' and the solo in 'Stone Cold', there are no complaints. New keyboard player David Rosenthal appears to have slotted into the position well enough and the band are airing one of the strongest Rainbow sets to date. The limelight is totally stolen by Ritchie though and at the end of the show he looks all set to smash his axe. Obviously the antics of von Arb are still in his mind and when he's just about to hurl his guitar against his amps he suddenly stops and tosses the complete instrument into the audience. It's a killer punch and one can't help but smile. Even Blackmore seems to be grinning as he takes hold of another Strat and proceeds to remove the strings one by one — he simply can't be outdone in the showmanship stakes. Definitely a night of top-notch metallic fun and games. Give me more!"

According to *Westerner World* in September 1982, the show in Lubbock, Texas was a disappointment for all concerned; "On the night of August 7th, three bands were scheduled to appear at the Municipal Auditorium: Rainbow, Saxon and Riot. Only Rainbow and Saxon came on stage. Riot did not appear because of differences between the band and the promoter. They were scheduled to appear at 7:30pm, but decided to wait until 8:00 in order to get more exposure by those who got to the concert late, thus, the promoter asked them to leave. Saxon then took the stage and 'put on a pretty good show' according to Dottie Townsend, Coliseum Auditorium Manager. Rainbow then came on, a half hour late, then went off after playing only three numbers without an encore. Townsend said that the band was in bad playing form, and eventually walked off because a few "fans" were throwing cups at them. Many fans were expecting to see a supposed great show, but ended up paying $9.00 for a very short and somewhat disappointing concert."

In August 1982, the *St Louis Post Dispatch* considered of the Busch Memorial Stadium performance; "It seems as if each edition of Rainbow is different. So it's difficult to keep track of the players. One thing for certain, though, is that lead guitarist Ritchie Blackmore has yet to achieve the same acclaim with this band as he had with Deep Purple. This is despite the fact that he has had some highly intelligent themes in his songs. The group opened with a heavy rock number that was impossible to decipher because the pounding of the two bass drums created an echo. But things quickly became better when the group moved into 'MISS Mistreated', and they stayed that way through the end of the set."

Notably, Rainbow wasn't always the headline act on their 1982 tour. Hart explained; "In mid August we played two big sold-out stadium shows in St Louis at The Busch Memorial Stadium and The Kansas City Arrowhead Stadium, not headlining, but as special guests to REO Speedwagon who were massive at the time having had a number one album, *Hi Fidelity*, in the US charts the year before."

Not that being the headliner was perhaps the be-all-and-end-all of course. In previous years, Blackmore and Powell had advocated that whether or not Rainbow should headline should be determined by the demand of each venue and that throughout one tour, it would be ideal if the option was interchangeable — whatever it took to bring in the crowds.

As Rainbow set their sights on international success, Hart recalled; "We arrived in Japan on October 10th, two days prior to playing three nights at the Festival Hall in Osaka as a prelude to a tramp round the country ending on 22nd with the obligatory two nights at The Budokan in Tokyo. Seven days and five thousand miles later we started the European leg in Oslo, Norway at the Drammenshallen supported by those infamous female rockers Girlschool."

Blackmore spoke highly of Girlschool as he told *Kerrang!*; "The girl (Denise Dufort on drums) really knows how to keep time. At first I thought to myself do I like them and do I give them the licence to make mistakes because of their feminity, but after a few dates it became apparent that they are in fact a good rock band."

A performance that took place in Finland was reviewed in *Sounds* in December 1982; "'Land Of Hope And Glory' makes for possibly the most emotive and powerful intro tape I can imagine, thundering out of the darkness before Judy Garland's disembodied voice announces 'we must be over the rainbow' and Blackmore's guitar oozes syrup into the heavy riff of 'Spotlight Kid', smoke bombs and sparklers joining the fast forward rhythm as giant mechanical eyeballs descend from the heavens beaming surrealistically in to the bowels of the quilt-coated crowd. That other prime Purple protagonist Roger Glover supplies bass lines in his silly hat which just leaves newest boy David Rosenthal, a classically trained organist, to complete the line-up."

"They're an impressive unit and though I must admit the obligatory ballad left me cold, my worst fears of an onstage pop bland-out were completely unrealised. Rainbow's massive jukebox hits are magnificently heavy live. Indeed the only bore of the evening was Dave's over-long organ solo — he's definitely at his best on the *Close Encounters*-style call and response passage with Blackmore, at the opening of 'Power'. Blackmore himself sparkles most brightly on the blues intro to 'Can't Happen Here' or the passage before 'All Night Long' with his guitar teasing and flirting like an LA street walker or swooping and attacking like a venom-crazed pterodactyl."

"But for my money the finest moment comes with their droog-approved reappraisal of Ludwig Van's 'Ode To Joy' which precedes the more populist set-closer 'Long Live Rock 'n' Roll'. The crowd bay desperately for more like a horde of hardened beer tasters facing a brewery strike and before long Blackmore's guitar rings out a beautiful melody from the darkness joined one by one by the other instruments until the guitar transmutes into the spine-tingling opening chords of 'Since You Been Gone', cut short after the first chorus for a more nostalgic retread of 'Smoke On The Water', a fearsome finale to a fine show."

Prior to doing a gig in Hamburg in November 1982, Blackmore told *Kerrang!*; "I like Hamburg as a town, it brings back many memories but as a gig, the audience seem a bit jaded, it's as if they've seen it all before and there's nothing worse than playing a gig where the first three rows have their arms crossed and stare blankly. It makes you feel a right twit running around the stage like some demented animal in front of a crowd of statues."

Of the performance in Hamburg, the *Kerrang!* journalist reported; "The girl backing singers climb up onto a platform that keeps them invisible from the paying onlookers while rock and roll's answer to Les Dawson, crew manager Raymond D'Addario, runs about the place doing last minute checks on the explosives and other effects rigged up around the place. As the voice of a young, virginal and undrugged Judy Garland recites the entree to her canine partner, the audiences eyes and ears are savagely bludgeoned by flash pots, and before anyone can regain a sensible semblance of hearing and vision the group are already on stage with Blackmore furiously belting out the opening chords of 'Spotlight Kid'."

"During the solo he whips his guitar into a frenzy with the lead while "Jolene" reveals a visionary side to his performance when spitting out the lyrics; 'just like a junkie you always want more,' he intones, simultaneously wrapping the mic lead around his arm like a tourniquet, making the gesture of someone about to fix up. Ever since Purple days the two obvious frontmen have been the vocalist and the guitarist (which is probably why the whole set-up eventually deteriorated — too many chiefs and not enough Indians), and "Jolene" has certainly displayed his worth in the singer/songwriter bracket taking the whole set-up to a new peak of success with some solid HR commerciality."

"It's only on stage that the criticisms come fast and furious, for Turner at times proves quite a schizophrenic personality going from the headstrong, powerful and dynamic to the whimpering, weaker realms of cabaret (making the likes of Charles Hawtrey look positively butch) within a matter of performances. This unpredictable personality change seems to affect the rest of the group's standard of playing, which in a way is understandable when you think that as a frontman, any embarrassment or cock up reflects on the rest of the mob."

"As you can imagine, Joe comes in line for the occasional scholarly slap on the back of the head. Glover, Rondinelli and Rosenthal, however, come over as being much more potent than just a set of accompanying players — especially the first two who've firmly affixed their distinguished personas into the Rainbow set-up."

"Glover now has a bass solo and occasionally whips out his tambourine for good measure, while Rondinelli goes to almost Muppet-like measures to get the fans frothing with some bare-fisted skin-beating, using his delightfully coiffured barnet to good effect (and before anyone starts an argument regarding who used this "bare fists" gimmick first — Aldridge or the Round One — the answer is in fact Don Brewer of Grand Funk)."

"Rosenthal still needs to inject some of his well-concealed fiery temperament into his performance which at the moment is a bit transparent — hardly surprising really as the ex-Boston preppy got thrown in at the deep end going from relative anonymity to mega-stardom in the space of one audition cassette. His soloing and improvisations are occasionally reminiscent of a more studious Tony Carey and the pup does actually get going when indulging in some blues interplay with Mr Blackmore, as ever the epitome of an axe hero continually teasing and cajoling his avid stargazers

Rainbow - *Straight Between The Eyes*: In-depth

and, although the group have strayed into more melodic musical spheres on vinyl, live his performance still hasn't lost the maniacal, moody, theatrical flair that puts this genius on the musical map. Tonight he isn't particularly hot, but still manages to raise a few temperatures with a steamin', stampeding version of 'Power' which should've been the single in Britain. He also includes a delightful diversion by playing a teasing snippet of 'Hey Joe' during 'Long Live Rock 'n' Roll'. There's no encore and definitely no apologies for the fact."

In December 1982, *Kerrang!* reported on a gig that took place in Berlin; "As one might (or might not) expect, the stiffness of the city doesn't reflect on the evenings' performance, which everybody agrees is one of the best of the last few. The audience certainly go for it and the band reciprocate by turning out an A-1 set. The show's probably enhanced by the fact that the size of the building allows for all props to be used and once one is confronted by a set of familiar, probing eyeballs that hover dangerously over the massed throng there's no turning back. A festive feast of highlights on the evening is given a welcome touch of icing courtesy of Blackmore's six-string sacrifice."

****

For those who missed the tour, an official video was released of the performance that took place in San Antonio on 18th of August. Titled *Live Between The Eyes*, the show documents the band playing incredibly well. Not only that, but it provides an insight into what the stage setup looked like around that time. The moving eyes as per the album art stay illuminated throughout. Technologically, the days of the temperamental many-bulbed rainbow — as seen on *Live In Munich 1977* —

were no more. The eyes didn't always behave though!

As Hart put it; "In San Antonio, the show was filmed for the video release *Live Between The Eyes*. This tour was, of course without the now long-gone, famous rainbow arch. The "centrepiece" was now two giant bloodshot eyes mimicking the *Straight Between The Eyes* album cover with two huge spotlights acting as the iris of each eye. Another great idea badly executed as some nights, when the eyes descended from behind the curtain up on the rig, the "eyes", (which were supposed to be synchronised to look left then right and beam straight out into the audience as one and look as if they were ripping out your soul), got an independent life of their own. Alas, they, hilariously, became "cross-eyes"; one would not work or would start winking. Ooooh, scary! Not quite the effect we were hoping for!"

Cooky Crawford opined about this gig on social media in 2017: "*Live Between The Eyes* shows Rainbow at their peak with this line-up, in my opinion. Joe had an incredible voice and range and was always in great vocal shape. Bobby was a powerhouse and also played better when people were watching. David was again in my opinion the best keyboard player in Rainbow and you could tell by the interaction with Ritchie. He loved playing back and forth with David as David was pitch-perfect and could mimic anything Ritchie came up with. Roger was the catalyst who held it all down and was a jack-of-all-trades and producer of the album. 'Spotlight Kid' opened the show with a bang and we used some pyrotechnics at the intro controlled by Raymond D'Addario."

"The eyes themselves were run by a tech from See Factor by the name of Sal Lupo who loved pointing them at the soundman (Gordon Patterson) and lighting tech (Tony Mazzuchi) just for laughs. Those eyes were stored while travelling in two cases the size of a Volkswagen Beetle and didn't fit through many a stage door, especially in Europe."

"We also had two beautiful background singers in Lin Robinson and Dee Beale who filled out the sound nicely."

Cooky also gave a great insight into the concert and of Rainbow's overall happenings around that time: "San Antonio was a great place to play and was known by the crew as the spandex capital of the world as the girls backstage were a great inspiration and came dressed to kill! Usually on shows like this where the band knew they were being filmed they would have been nervous, but everyone looks very relaxed here and the playing was very good. Before the show, in the tuning room Ritchie would be loosening up by kicking soccer balls and exercising his fingers, playing his usual favourite things like the Brandenburg Concertos and such. He also used to drink Johnnie Walker Black and Coke to an imaginary line on the bottle where he knew he got a nice buzz going. Ritchie did suffer from stage fright in a way as he knew all eyes would be on him and this was a lot of pressure for one person to handle."

"The new songs from *Straight Between The Eyes* came off beautifully, especially 'Tearin' Out My Heart'. When it came time for 'Kill The King' you can see the smash-up guitar (a Strat-imitation with the maple neck) was fitted with a black Fender pickup in the treble position and I had scalloped the neck so Ritchie enjoyed playing it before he went about smashing it to pieces. I got so good at keeping them in tune like his main guitars that he could play them for quite a while before laying them to waste."

"His main guitars never went out of tune on stage and he only switched from number one to number two for a deeper, heavier sound and this was done at the break in Beethoven's Ninth as he came back out on stage for his solo. I also used to give him more preamp during solos by turning up the input on his Aiwa tape deck and you can see him motion to me with his hands in a circular motion on 'Spotlight Kid' on this tape."

"I could tell he was enjoying himself here and his amps sounded hot this night. Since tube amps can be affected by temperature and humidity their sound could change drastically. We were trying to change his tubes once a week on whatever head he was using most often and we would experiment with them when he'd show up for a soundcheck. He didn't always come to soundcheck so he relied on me to make sure it was sounding good. I usually stuck to whatever amp he was playing the night before. His amps always sounded best when they were about to blow their resistors, so I had to keep my eyes on them and used to stand behind them watching their orange glow. When he played, the intensity would show in the glow of those KT88s. I used to keep a record of when the tubes were changed in each of his three Marshall Major heads he used. The tubes were hard to come by in those days and were very expensive. As far as I know there were no overdubs done on it. This was a very honest example of Rainbow at their best."

Live Between The Eyes is an excellent example of how yes, Rainbow had gone commercial by this point but it wasn't to the extent that their live performances no longer included Blackmore's spellbinding guitar work. Sure, the solos are less extended than they were previously, but the band overall sound fantastic together. Even in the absence of Glover's thoughtful production on stage, the sound is cohesive and high quality.

Turner shows that he is a versatile singer who can handle a range of contrasting styles, proving to those who are doubtful about this era of Rainbow that really, what is there not to like? Glover and Rondinelli on rhythm play seamlessly and

Rondinelli's solo is fun, played with humour and engaging. A true professional despite his young age, Rosenthal plays with ease and with style.

The setlist that features on the video includes classics from the Dio and Bonnet years ('Long Live Rock 'n' Roll' and 'All Night Long' respectively) as well as the Deep Purple classic, 'Smoke On The Water'.

Overall, Blackmore's choice of band line-up and their execution of a varied and enjoyable setlist is demonstrative of a highpoint in Rainbow's tenure.

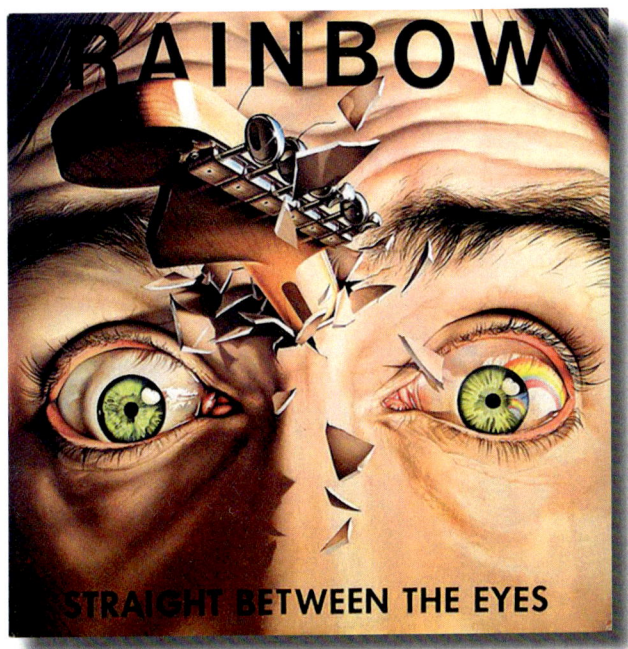
UK

Japan

The album cover had virtually nothing in the way of variations but of course the Japanese version included an obi which contained information such as track titles.

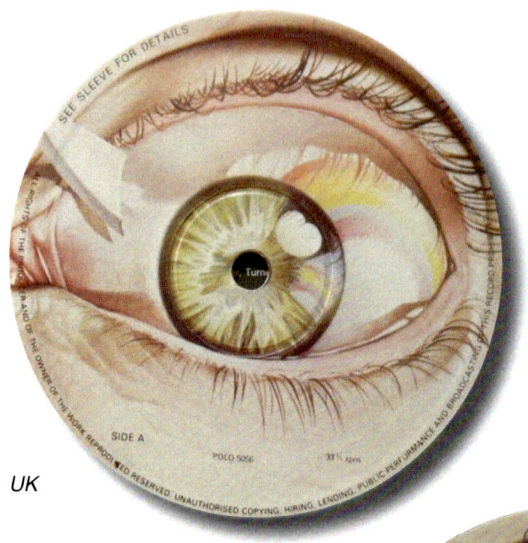

UK

Even though there were no cover variations, there were label variations. Custom labels had become the norm by the early eighties and were used in most countries, but with variations in the text. For example, the UK version didn't include the song titles at all whilst some countries opted for a more traditional-looking design.

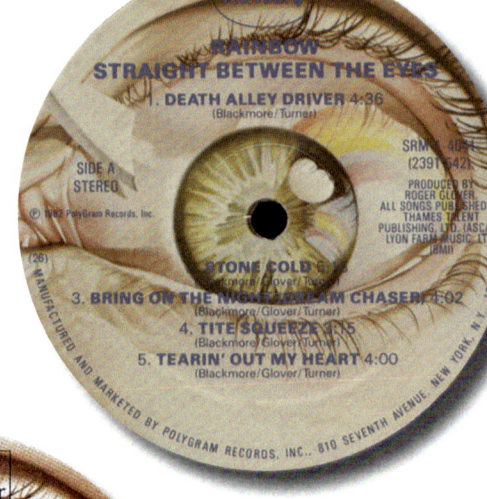

USA

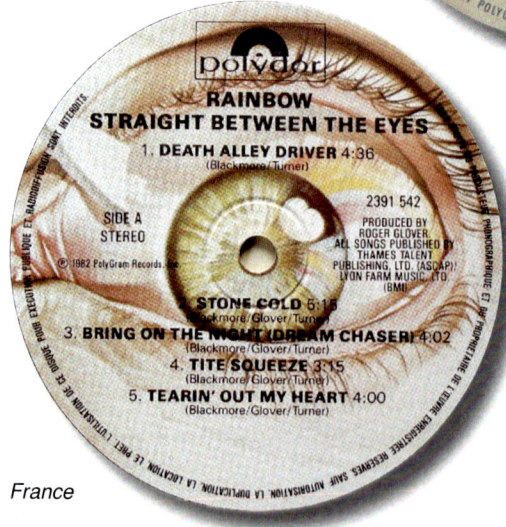

France

Germany

New Zealand

Yugoslavia

Cassette covers

USA

USA club edition

Australia

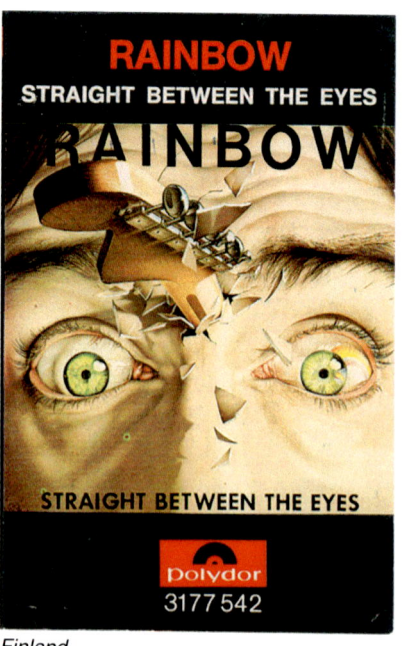

Finland

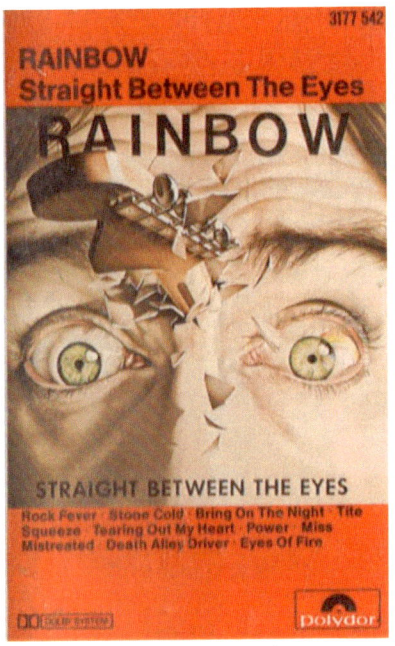

Germany

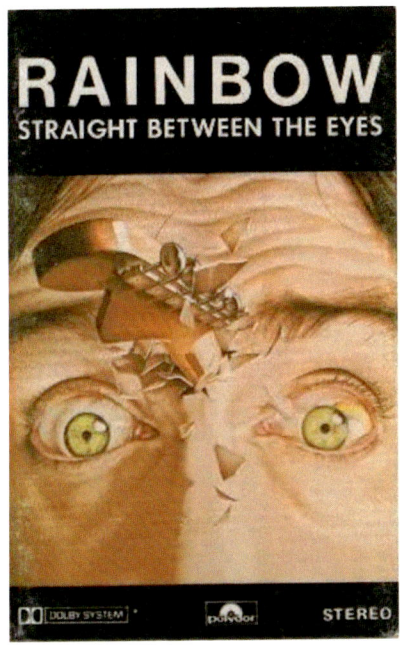

Spain

South Korea

France

The US was still clinging on to the 8-track cartridge format.

UK

Italy

Japan

Most countries were given the radio-friendly 'Stone Cold' as the single. It was a hit in the UK but it didn't reach the heights of 'I Surrender'.

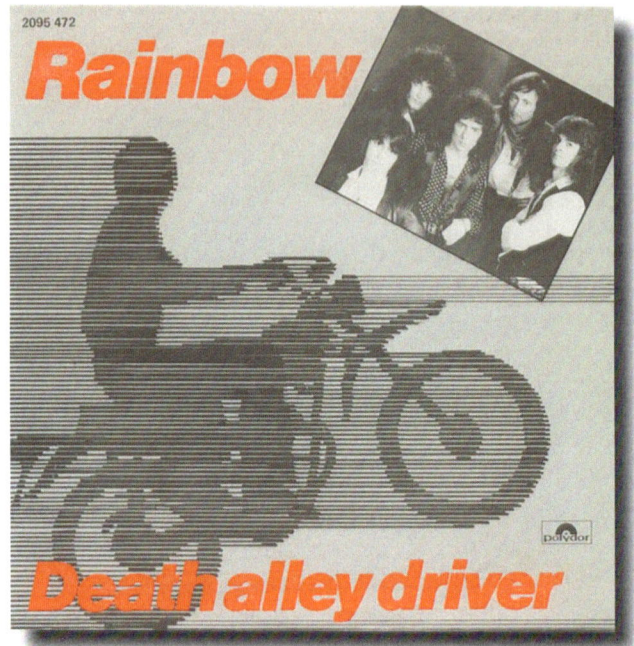

Netherlands

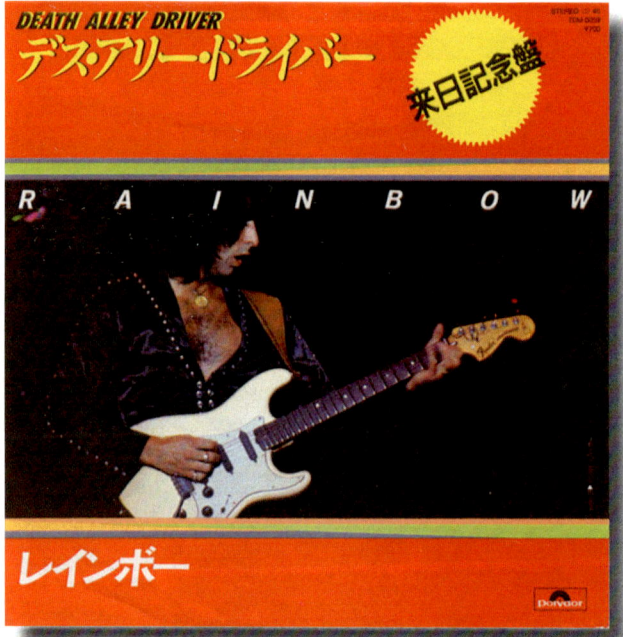

Japan

'Death Alley Driver' made for an excellent single but the song was only released in such format in just three countries: Japan, Netherlands… and Bolivia, where it was backed with 'Eyes Of Fire'. The Dutch cover left a lot to be desired but the Japanese one – as is so often the case – had a more attractive design.

Chapter Four
Legacy

With touring to promote *Straight Between The Eyes* complete, there was a feeling of uncertainty within Rainbow. Rumours of a Deep Purple reunion had been doing the rounds in the music press and although conflicting accounts had been given from various sources, it was no secret that Rainbow's future wasn't guaranteed.

Although the reunion rumours were public knowledge and even though Blackmore himself had spoken of his interest in such, it didn't come across as a certainty. For instance, Ian Gillan was quoted in *Billboard* in November 1983; "We've talked about it quite a few times, all sorts of different combinations. Ritchie Blackmore asked me to join Rainbow at one time, and then over the years it was talked about, but it fell to pieces for various reasons, mostly because of the management. When the musicians were involved it was fine, really, but then it got fragmented. Nobody is now involved with the original Deep Purple management at all, but they own the name, all that sort of thing."

In December 1982, when asked if he would ever consider a Deep Purple reunion, Blackmore told *Sounds*; "Yeah, I might do that. In fact we might be talking about it in the near future. But it'd have to be done for the right reasons. A lot of people I talk to would like to see the band again but we wouldn't be recording live triple albums or anything like that. I don't believe in doing it just for the money. I'd do it with the right line-up — Roger, Ian, Jon and Gillan. And if it worked out we might do a creative studio album. It'd be fun, but I wouldn't like it to interfere with Rainbow."

He didn't regret leaving Deep Purple though. He said in the same interview; "I'm very pleased I left when I did, it was great to go then because the band had started to go on the slide. David and the rest had started going very souly. I wanted a rock 'n' roll band, not a funky soul band."

Just as well really considering the creative journey that Blackmore was able to go on with Rainbow. Besides, would something like 'Stargazer' or even 'Death Alley Driver' have been songs that Blackmore would have been able to persuade Glenn Hughes and/or David Coverdale to do with him? Quite possibly not.

Although many people would go on to be delighted about the reunion of Deep Purple mark two, it is certainly surreal to think of all the amazing music that wouldn't have been had Blackmore not left Deep Purple in spring 1975 to go and start Rainbow.

With Rainbow, Blackmore had achieved what he'd set out to do in terms of the reasons he had stated upon leaving Deep Purple in 1975: he wanted more creative and commercial control of a band that was his own.

With everything still up in the air after *Straight Between The Eyes* though, Rainbow took a short break. According to Colin Hart, everyone was concerned that the future of the band wasn't something to take for granted: "The tour over, with surprisingly no British dates, those band members and crew who were US residents, returned home to Connecticut for Christmas and an uncertain future for some. The tour, though on the surface successful, had not pushed Rainbow to the supergroup stature that Ritchie expected and demanded. He was very quiet on the return flight, deep in private

Legacy

conversation with Bruce. Would the inevitable Yuletide team changes be made once more, I asked myself, as 1983 approached? Ritchie, in a rare moment of indecision decided to come off the road while he thought his future through. Bruce, having no short-term plan for the band decided to "lay off" Joe, David and Bobby indefinitely which didn't go down too well, but it was better that way than giving them false hope."

In December 1982, Blackmore told *Sounds*; "At the moment I'm going through a phase of self evaluation. So I've been putting off recording plans. There's supposed to be a new album in April but we won't be doing it until we've got the ideas. I think in a sense we've lost direction, but at the same time I was quite pleased with the last two albums' melodic vein. I'd like the next one to be as good, if not better, but after you've done twenty albums it gets much harder to constantly improve... I never listen to my own stuff. I was in a record shop the other day and I heard an old Purple album — it was a really weird feeling. At the moment I'm lacking a lot of motivation. I practice a lot and I still love to play guitar but I'm not sure where I want to be, whether it's in the Foreigner field or hard rock, it varies from day to day. You see I'm losing interest in heavy rock just for the sake of it — I refuse to play heavy just for the sake of it like, say, AC/DC do. There has to be some sort of subtlety as well. There's no one I look towards for inspiration now. I'm bored with looking towards Hendrix. I find myself listening to Tull, though obviously that's not a direction Rainbow will go in, and Abba. I love Abba's heavy classical progressions, they're brilliant writers. I respect Jeff Beck, he was probably the best rock 'n' roll guitarist in the Yardbirds days — but he wants to get away from rock 'n' roll now."

Upon being asked if he'd written much in the way of new

material by that point, Blackmore said in the same interview; "No. When I'm on the road I tend to become a bit of a zombie, I'm only creative at home, and I'll be at home all December so hopefully by January there'll be some good material. But I refuse to just go in the studio and bang something out to satisfy the record company's plans. When I left Purple one of the biggest things I wanted in my new deal was a maximum of one album a year. In Purple they wanted us to do three a year that's why every other one was sub-standard."

It's a shame to think that the future was looking so uncertain after everything Rainbow had achieved with *Straight Between The Eyes* and after everything that Joe Lynn Turner had done for the band. In particular, one only has to look at the writing credits on *Difficult To Cure* and *Straight Between The Eyes* to ascertain that even though Rainbow was very much Blackmore's band, Turner contributed to an undeniable extent.

In all fairness though, it seems that upon joining Rainbow, everyone in it was always very wary that the job might not be the most permanent anyway. Turner told *Kerrang!*; "I'm not saying we couldn't be axed tomorrow and a whole new Rainbow brought in. But everything seems to be going smoothly and I think you can sense it on the new album. There's an honesty there — a passion! We actually like the people we're with and I hate to say it but, yes, we're enjoying ourselves."

To say that the frequent line-up changes in Rainbow were always an outcome of something negative though would certainly be unfair. Understandably, all musicians had to bring their A-game if they wanted to join — and indeed stay in — Rainbow.

In an interview with *Hit Krant* in December 1982, Glover was asked of Blackmore, "Will you deny that he has a big ego?" His response: "I do. He is only demanding and that is his right. If you, as a musician in Rainbow, do not give everything that is in you, you better leave. This has often happened in the past. Ritchie hates people who want to be in Rainbow only for the big bucks or the ego tripping. He is smart enough to see that and those guys are the first to fly out."

In May 1982, Glover told *Cleveland Scene*; "It's always difficult to come up with the right combinations of musicians, especially in a band like Rainbow. They have a reputation of going through musicians like other people go through marriages... I think a lot of the changes going on with the band are because he hasn't found the kind of band he wants to work with live. You can have a good player, but that doesn't say he's gonna fit well in the band. Ritchie demands a certain feedback. He's excellent himself, and he expects excellence from his players. Finding that right bunch of people is difficult, but I think we're pretty close to it right now."

And of course, from 1979 onwards, the working rapport between Blackmore and Glover remained strong. Glover told *Kerrang!*; "In a way Ritchie's too good. He tends to do things very technically but, for me, musical ability is the least important factor. The most important thing, I think, is to communicate with an audience and you can sometimes say more in a scream than you can in the most articulate, well-sung piece. I like to see Ritchie just open out and let loose. Sometimes when he's tuning up he plays the most brilliant things, then when he actually comes to a solo they're not there. Of course they can be, it just requires a lot of talking. There have been occasions when he was totally at a loss to know what to do and I've just said the right thing."

Kerrang! commented; "When Roger first assumed the

Rainbow - *Straight Between The Eyes*: In-depth

mantle of Rainbow's producer his prime intention was to bring Ritchie's guitar to the forefront of the band's sound but, with *Down To Earth* finally emerging as an overt attempt to be commercial and expand the band's following, Strat attack was sacrificed and song content pushed to the fore. With *Straight Between The Eyes*, however, the Blackmore guitar once again has its safety catch removed and with Joe Lynn Turner now fully invoked on the writing front, the sort of hooks the band previously relied on Ballard to produce are slowly starting to filter through. Coupling an all-enveloping commercial quality with a near-Purplesque dynamism, Rainbow has shifted course, subtly yet strongly. Vision as ever sharpened by hindsight, Roger still sees room for improvement but generally he's pleased with the overall sound and feel, something that hasn't been true before."

Despite the temptation of a Deep Purple mark two reunion, although the determining factors are unclear, Blackmore and co. would go on to make one more Rainbow album with Turner at the helm as their vocalist. The decision would see Rainbow go to Sweet Silence Studios in Copenhagen in May 1983 to record *Bent Out Of Shape*. Released in the autumn, the album got to number eleven in the UK and to number thirty-four in the US.

Kerrang! reviewed *Bent Out Of Shape* in September 1983; "Hark! Listen to the dulcet tones of the Rainbow. Dig deep into the pockets, dispense with the necessary readies and prepare to be blown away! Yeah, this new Rainbow release follows *Straight Between The Eyes* as one excellent piece of plastic — it's thumbs up from me... But beware those of you who've just put the needle to *Rising* for the 8,000th time, while *Bent Out Of Shape* should indeed blow you away, it sure as hell ain't gonna cave your face in at the same time! Y'see, as Ritchie Blackmore has been hinting for a good three years now, he certainly couldn't give a toss about being recognised as the world's greatest axe exponent anymore — at least not on vinyl. Nah, sensible chap that he is, Ritchie wants to be part of a group that's producing class rock 'n' roll — no more, no less."

"For a guy with such a supposedly huge ego, he ain't letting it show through his Strat! Blackmore's breaks are short, concise, to the point and as such far more effective than five-minute ramblings. Even the album's two instrumentals, 'Anybody There' and 'Snowman' are tunes in their own right, just as they should be! Songs should be the key to anyone's heart and some sizeable locks could be opened here. With memorable moments in force, a weekend's spinning has been totally rewarding, revealing possibly Rainbow's most complete work to date. There's very little emphasis on performing to the standards required of a hard rock/heavy metal band, more in coming up with marvellous music and believe it or not, Rainbow mark eighty-seven (is it?) are infinitely superior when they keep it calm, keep it stealthy and don't worry too much about "rockin' out"."

"You'll get the drift when you compare newer-sounding Rainbow to older guard material. The former has produced two of this year's finest tunes, a double-headed delight on side B of this disc. 'Desperate Heart' stands out as the biggie, Joe Lynn Turner proving he's got as much in him as Lou Gramm (a compliment indeed!), while David Rosenthal shows that he has the necessary keyboard subtleties that are needed in this more mature Rainbow."

"Instant yet lasting, totally contemporary and a sophisticated joy to the ears — as is 'Street Of Dreams', the latest single criminally insulted by Chris Welch, taking up where 'Stone Cold' left off and carrying the style pretty much to ultimate perfection. Then there's 'Stranded', a

Rainbow - *Straight Between The Eyes*: In-depth

spacey, keyboard-dominated opener that caresses you into submission. 'Can't Let You Go', where Joe Lynn Turner reveals his increasingly mature and sensitive lyrical capabilities, and 'Fool For The Night', a Blackmore/Turner composition which is as close to definitive modern day Rainbow as anything. Minor quibbles concern 'Fire Dance' and 'Make Your Move', more on the old Rainbow pulse but too uninspired for such a generally well-crafted album, and also the fact that drummer Chuck Bürgi hasn't been given the chance to really shine here. (Refer to Balance's 'In For The Count' for a true reflection of his capabilities and quality). Minor quibbles indeed in terms of overall quality control. Now if Rainbow can carry that inspired atmosphere to the stage we'll all be laughing — even Mr Blackmore might have to let a smile out. *Bent Out Of Shape*? Nah, Rainbow have trained hard — and they're in better shape than ever!"

It was also reviewed in *Sounds*; "*Bent Out Of Shape* is a beast of many moods, a mouth-watering multi-layered muesli of tempos and textures. Richer and more satisfying than *Straight Between The Eyes*, it recalls elements of *Rainbow Rising* as well as the later jukebox-rock that took Ritchie back to *Top Of The Pops*. Rock fans who can appreciate class as well as raw power will be well-served by this platter. Sure, there's plenty of melodic sensibility in evidence — but the crucial point is mass appeal doesn't necessarily equate with blandness."

"Some people make it into an art form and Blackmore could well be one of them. Crafty old Ritchie has found his top form again here, demonstrating with breathtaking ease why he, like so few others, genuinely deserves the epithet "Guitar Hero". Even at its gentlest, the album still sparkles thanks to his superb guitar playing. The lobotomised Schenker should do himself a favour and check it out, it's proof positive that longevity doesn't have to equate with going through the motions."

"Blackmore's fretboard forays never sound tired or clichéd. There's real feeling here. The difference between *Bent Out Of Shape* and the recent MSG abortion is the difference between Liverpool FC and Gillingham FC. Style, class, depth, you name it, this has got it. Lovers of more unrestrained music can shelter in the storms of the gloriously Purple-esque 'Fire Dance' and the full-frontal gallop of 'Make Your Move', both blessed with hair raising guitar holocausts. And let's not forget 'Drinking With The Devil', a savagely satanic-saunter whose deliciously clichéd lyrics betray a worrying carefree attitude towards boozing with Beelzebub. I had a similar experience in a strip bar with Edwin Pouncey once, but I digress."

"Lovers of the less hectic will find solace in 'Anybody There', with Blackmore supplying gorgeous guitar over a Bach-like backing (guaranteed to become an air guitarists delight) that proves once again that his Bach is no worse than his Beethoven (and that's fairly stunning too). Similarly breath taking is the guitar break midway into the toe-tappingly tasty 'Desperate Heart', which soars and spirals into some head-tuning high-pitched yelps."

"Elsewhere we get Ritchie's interpretation of Howard Blake's 'Snowman'. Beginning like Jon And Vangelis on mandrax, its morosely dreamy feel is rudely awakened by a wonderfully reckless guitar burst. Finally, there's the battery of well-crafted "radio rock" — the addictive pump of the opener 'Stranded' with its populist punch-the-air chants, the more up-tempo 'Fool For The Night' and of course 'Street Of Dreams' — not quite 'I Surrender' but eminently listenable all the same."

"And that just leaves 'Can't Let You Go' with its great

Rainbow - *Straight Between The Eyes*: In-depth

Dave Rosenthal opening organ, a sombre and majestic passage that sounds like a genuine church organ and precedes the classy contagious cruise of the song proper. This is obviously the one for Ritchie's Vincent Price impersonations. As you can tell, most of the many faces of Rainbow are represented in ship-shape form. Indeed, there is not a bald patch on the album. Glover's production is as faultless as the playing, it will sell in droves both sides of the Atlantic, and it proves once again that the name of Blackmore is synonymous with quality."

And in *Melody Maker*; "Let me take you back to last week's singles review and Dee Snider sounding off about Rainbow's new forty five 'Street Of Dreams': 'This is NOT Rainbow. This is just another band in a long line of pseudo-Foreigner, washed down heavy metal rock 'n' roll bands.' Mr Snider may not be the most tactful of earthlings, but one thing is for certain he sure doesn't bullshit or beat (the meat?) around the bush when it comes to upfront retribution."

"Rainbow sure need some heavy wrist slapping this time around and I'm real glad that I've got Dee on my side. Unfortunately this LP is a virtual testament to the downfall of Ritchie Blackmore and his never ending Rainbow. Sad but true. A detailed history lesson of the last few albums would prove the point adequately, but is rather unnecessary as every self-respecting Rainbow fan (past or present) will realise that the band peaked with *Rainbow Rising* and have slid backwards since. 'Stranded' kicks off side one and — surprise, surprise — what do we find but vocalist Joe Lynn Turner turning in his most successful Lou Gramm impression to date over a sub (new age) Blackfoot-style song. Good radio rock for sure, but this could be any one of ten bands."

"'Can't Let You Go' weighs in as a mean and moody mid-paced strutter much in the mould of a faster 'Stone Cold' rework. Oh, a special mention to David Rosenthal's excellent gothic inspired keyboard intro. In fact, this young tinkler turns in some very tasty ivory frills throughout the LP. 'Fool For The Night' actually hints back at pre-*Down To Earth* style Rainbow, and 'Firedance' actively displays *Rainbow Rising* roots. In fact, Joe Lynn Turner (the Mike Yarwood of heavy metal?) adopts a distinct Ronnie James Dio vocal stance. The whole song is very similar in structure to 'A Light In The Black', one of Rainbow's classic songs. Full marks, but only for this one."

"Side two (the weaker incidentally) is introduced by 'Desperate Heart', a rather nondescript song saved only by Rosenthal's superb keyboard twists and some tasty (almost modern) sound effects. 'Street Of Dreams' sucks (see Dee Snider's reasons); it's not a good ballad by any stretch of the imagination and the melody is terminally irritating."

"The lynch pin, or filler, or throwaway (delete as applicable) comes in the shape of 'Drinking With The Devil', a full frontal rocker short on imagination and skill — Raven can do this sort of stuff much better. Written by Howard Blake and interpreted by Blackmore, 'Snowman' is a very moody instrumental that works exceptionally well. Again the keyboards shine through fantastically, fully complementing Blackmore's guitar virtuosity. The closer, 'Make Your Move', is another full tilt rocker but crafted much more effectively than the others on this LP. A rather bleak and dismal ending to a rather bleak LP, I'm afraid. Ritchie Blackmore is still searching for that pot of gold and every time he releases a new album, he moves one step closer to total sell-out. Come on Ritchie, let's get back to basics."

Despite the mixed reviews overall, if the main objective of *Bent Out Of Shape* was to appeal to an audience in the US, it could be argued that it was a case of mission accomplished.

Rainbow - *Straight Between The Eyes*: In-depth

In October 1983, Glover told *Melody Maker*; "The way you sell more records is to break America, and the way you break America is to get played on American radio. People say the band's gone soft, or gone commercial, but that's bullshit. The band has survived."

Billboard reviewed the album in September 1983; "The title suggests another headbanging extravaganza from Ritchie Blackmore's hard rock quintet, but here Rainbow takes a surprising, if familiar, new stylistic turn. Blackmore and chief writing partner Joe Lynn Turner, the band's vocalist, contribute songs in a more melodic pop/rock vein closer to Foreigner and Journey than Rainbow's usual peer group, while bassist Glover gives the production a crisp, sleek finish likewise aimed at AOR traditionalists. Songs like 'Stranded' and 'Can't Let You Go' could reap new airplay dividends as a result."

As did *Cash Box*; "As one of the prime proponents of pop-metal, Rainbow had a number of hits in the late seventies and early eighties, and continues its grand headbanging tradition with this LP of punchy hard rock. Though the album is filled with the standard axe riffs and incessant drumbeats that characterise the metallic mode, the lyrics on such numbers as 'Fire Dance' and 'Stranded' rise high above the typical brainbashing fare. Other key tunes include the axe-ellent Blackmore instrumental 'Anybody There' and the raucous 'Drinking With The Devil'."

Rainbow's 1983 tour programme advocated; "Having spent much of 1983 hard at work in the studios, Rainbow are finally back on the road with the brand new *Bent Out Of Shape* LP, which is by far their strongest album to date and proves beyond all doubt that they're still one of the major forces in the rock world. While cuts like 'Stranded', 'Desperate Heart' and 'Fool For The Night' affirm that Blackmore and his band can still rock with a vengeance, cleverly worked tunes like 'Street Of Dreams' and 'Can't Let You Go' show that there's definitely more to their music than your basic straightforward "crash-bang-wallop" heavy metal."

Glover said, "We finished touring in December '82 and then we spent the first couple of months of the new year getting initial ideas for the new record together. In March we started rehearsing for a couple of months and during those rehearsals most of the ideas took shape. In fact I think this is the first album where we've gone into the studio quite so prepared. Usually, a lot of stuff gets written in the studio. But I think being prepared worked quite well because it allowed us to concentrate more on performance rather than writing. We started recording at Sweet Silence Studios in Copenhagen at the beginning of May."

"Originally we'd planned to go back to Le Studio in Canada, where we did *Straight Between The Eyes*, but unfortunately that was booked. So rather than face somewhere we hadn't been before we decided to go to a place that we knew (*Difficult To Cure* was recorded at Sweet Silence in 1980). And Copenhagen is especially good for Ritchie and also the drum sound — but, more importantly, for Ritchie... I personally consider *Bent Out Of Shape* as being very much a progression for Rainbow and I think it's also important to mention the arrival of Chuck Bürgi (ex-Hall & Oates, Balance, and Aldo Nova) on drums. To me, the whole thing has a much more modern approach. It sounds like an eighties album as opposed to a throwback to the seventies kind of heavy metal thing. There'll always be an element of that because Ritchie's basically a heavy metal guitarist, and he'll always write music in a certain way, but I think the songs are evolving in a much more modern manner."

Even though *Bent Out Of Shape* was a strong album in

and of itself and boasted the singles, 'Street Of Dreams' and 'Can't Let You Go', 1984 would see Blackmore abandon Rainbow to dedicate his talents to the highly anticipated reunion of Deep Purple mark two.

It's a shame to consider that *Bent Out Of Shape* was the last album made with Turner in Rainbow, especially in view of the working rapport he had with Blackmore. The vocalist told *Goldmine* in 2008; "On 'Street Of Dreams' Ritchie came in after I sang the vocal — I had a really great moment on that song, obviously. He said, 'I can't play the lead. I'm intimidated.' I said, 'What?' He said, 'Your vocal is spot on.' I said, 'It is a good vocal and it is just what we believe in with others lives and reincarnation.' I broke open two Heinekens and I said, 'You go in there. This is our creation; this is our baby.' He lit the candles and got in the mood but he rose to the occasion. He came out and said, 'Cheers mate. Thanks for the inspiration'."

It seems that Deep Purple's reunion had been a long time coming. That is to say that no matter what Rainbow did after *Straight Between The Eyes*, perhaps really, there was little that could be done to ensure the continuation of Rainbow after that point.

Hart recalled; "Bruce had always kept in touch with Phil Banfield, Ian Gillan's personal manager and more than once I heard the rumour around the office that the two of them were "in a huddle" over, if not a complete reunion of Deep Purple, at least a one-off concert with the fabled line-up... The rumours of a Purple reunion persisted until March when Ritchie told me he would have one last attempt at breaking Rainbow. I was mystified as we were a massive draw in most markets, were we not already "broken"? Just what was he after? The albums, although not triple platinum, still sold in considerable number and the tours were always pretty much sold out in most venues. He had the respect of virtually every musician you could shake a stick at and Bruce had ensured his personal wealth was not only intact, but also expanding. In truth, he was not exactly unhappy, more restless and ill at ease. I guess the word was "unfulfilled".."

Regarding Hart's comment that Rainbow's albums were not selling in a way that made them platinum, it is worth nothing that *Straight Between The Eyes* eventually went silver in the UK.

To say that the reunion of Deep Purple mark two was a negative occurrence would certainly be an oversight. *Perfect Strangers* and the tour that followed it did incredibly well. Nevertheless, one can't help but wonder what another Rainbow album might have sounded like if it were made straight after the success of *Bent Out Of Shape*.

Another interesting point is that although Blackmore was funding Rainbow out of his own pocket and although the band still wasn't reaching the same commercial heights that had been the case with Deep Purple in the seventies, to say that Rainbow was underachieving would be frankly, inaccurate.

What Blackmore and Turner achieved as a writing partnership was incredible, as is clear in tracks such as 'Death Alley Driver' and 'Street Of Dreams'. It is understandable as to why despite the controversy of when Turner joined Deep Purple for their *Slaves And Masters* album (1990), there were still plenty of fans who were pleased to see Blackmore and Turner working together again — especially in view of the fact that Deep Purple mark two hadn't, by their own admission, gelled together well as a team when making *The House Of Blue Light* (1987).

And the legacy of *Straight Between The Eyes*? Well, to brush it off as simply a footnote to the era of when "Blackmore sold out and went commercial" would be a real shame. Sure,

Rainbow - *Straight Between The Eyes*: In-depth

Straight Between The Eyes isn't *Rainbow Rising*, but it certainly wasn't trying to be.

Essentially, *Straight Between The Eyes* was of its time in the sense of where Blackmore and indeed the rest of Rainbow were at when they made it. The same could be said for everything that Blackmore does now with his band, Blackmore's Night; it's not *Machine Head*, it's not Rainbow's debut album but to try comparing them, really, would be like trying to compare apples and oranges. Arguably, every album made stands up in its own right in the context of the time it was made and what the creative and commercial goals were as part of that.

Besides, across the range of musical genres that Blackmore has embraced throughout his career, he has often been candid about how he prefers playing live to working in the studio.

He told *Circus* in May 1982; "Though I hate to record, I enjoy performing live. I'm usually very drunk when I play. Part of me is shy, and I have to drink a lot to come out of myself. I do stay in control; I just like to have a good time playing. But I don't like to glamorise everything. I don't even like to do too many theatrics. Of course, it wouldn't work for us to go out with lutes and play Elizabethan melodies, as much as we might be tempted to. We have to put on a show. But all I do on the guitar is to emulate classical violin, which takes from sixteenth and seventeenth century organ music. The organ is so commanding — as opposed to guitar, just whimpering along."

Kerrang! considered in April 1982; "The fact no two studio LPs have been recorded by the same line-up has inevitably made a natural album-to-album progression that much harder. But, despite chops and changes, the band has developed with the new blood transfusions keeping live performances fresh and spontaneous (meaning shows veer wildly between the good and the bad) and the quota of new ideas consistently high."

"With the arrival of Roger Glover as producer and bassist in 1979, a watershed in Rainbow's history, the direction became at once more commercial and more clearly charted. The recording of *Down To Earth* and, more specifically, the Ballard-penned 'Since You Been Gone' put an end to cultish appeal and, in financial terms, made the future of the band considerably more secure. For some, equating speed with power and chart status with sell-out, this was sacrilege."

"The Rainbow's end with not a crock of gold in sight. Would Ritchie really play 'Since You Been Gone' live? The answer, of course, was yes and not only that but the shift away from the sombre, sultry heaviness of *Rainbow Rising*, rather than being a temporary hiccup, was continued firstly on *Difficult To Cure* and now on the new *Straight Between The Eyes*, a title recalling the way an exultant Jeff Beck first described Hendrix to Blackmore."

"While *Difficult To Cure* could have stood a little more of the man in black and a little less of Airey, his rather dated keyboards being the album's weak link, *Straight Between The Eyes*, recorded digitally (no less) at a studio just outside Montreal with his replacement David Rosenthal, is more balanced — a fine blend of the commercial, the aggressive and the epic, reflecting a rare new harmony within the band. Rising to the demands of a tight song structure, Blackmore now favours a more concise approach; one that tailors itself to the requirements of each individual song, while Joe Lynn Turner too has improved his performance. Though far from dry-throated on *Difficult To Cure*, his voice now has an added strength and depth, be he beating his chest on the up-tempo strutters ('Power', 'Rock Fever') or sweeping up the pieces of a broken heart ('Stone Cold', 'Tearin' Out My Heart')."

Straight Between The Eyes has a lot going for it in terms of how it is a great blend of hard rock and melodic vocal lines. Although some of the songs on it are less complex than others, on the whole, the strength of the album rests on some of the more iconic tracks such as 'Death Alley Driver', 'Stone Cold' and 'Eyes Of Fire'. Then of course there is the ballad in 'Tearin' Out My Heart', the straight up rock in 'Rock Fever' and the commerciality of 'Power'. It all bodes well for an enjoyable listening experience with plenty of replay value.

Although *Straight Between The Eyes* was shaped around that fact that Blackmore was aiming for commercial success, that's not to say that it is lacking in ideas. And those ideas were shaped by experienced, versatile musicians. There is a lot to be embraced in that regard.

Of course, in terms of the commercial aims that Blackmore was mindful of when making *Straight Between The Eyes*, the album doesn't feature the same extensive amount of soloing that fans had come to expect from the likes of his live performances with Deep Purple and indeed the Dio era of Rainbow. It's understandable as to why *Straight Between The Eyes* didn't do it for all of Blackmore's fans but does that make the songs on the album to be of lesser value? (I would argue that it doesn't but really, I'd like to leave this question as a rhetorical one).

In April 1982, Blackmore told *Kerrang!*; "I used to play a million notes a second when I was eighteen, twenty, and I found that I wasn't going anywhere. There was no fulfilment. Now I find I deliberately slow myself down; so much so that it's difficult to play fast. The other night I was playing at my fastest and found it a strain, but I know that's what kids want to see. The latest craze is who's the fastest."

Kerrang! asserted; "It's clear that at present Blackmore

is content and feeling considerably more fulfilled than in the days of *Rainbow Rising*."

To which he was quoted; "I was very angry at that time and I just wanted to get something out of my system. But by the time I got to *Long Live Rock 'n' Roll*, it had all gone and I suddenly thought where do I go from here? I guess the older you become the more you get into melodies. I can't stand just knocking out three chords, the AC/DC effect, that doesn't move me at all, which is no reflection on them. I'm classically orientated, a good strong melody with a strong metal feel is my ultimate aim and it's difficult because rock 'n' roll is limited usually to three or four chords so they're all you've got to produce different melodies. It can be done but when I was in Britain a couple of weeks ago a lot of the heavy metal I heard was just a racket. There was no thought behind it, it was just a case of turning up the amps. It seems popular though, which is good because if I thought reggae was in I'd probably give up. I can't stand reggae."

Regarding the legacy of the individual songs on *Straight Between The Eyes*, Turner has done the most in terms of keeping that alive. He has performed 'Death Alley Driver' and 'MISS Mistreated' as part of a number of his live shows in recent years alongside other such classics from his time in Rainbow: 'Jealous Lover', 'Can't Let You Go' and 'Street Of Dreams'. To this day, Turner acknowledges that his time in Rainbow was a pivotal point upon which his career escalated to new heights and his recent performances of some of the songs he did with Rainbow clearly show that he believed in them then and he believes in them now — surely testament to how when he was in Rainbow, he was singing with conviction.

In November 2015 Blackmore announced that he would be touring with a new line-up of Rainbow. With Ronnie Romero on vocals, the majority of songs in the setlist consisted of Deep Purple numbers and Rainbow ones from the Dio era. From the Bonnet era, 'Since You Been Gone' has been performed and from the Turner era, 'I Surrender' and 'Spotlight Kid'.

Overall, even though Turner perhaps speaks the most highly of *Straight Between The Eyes* today, there is no denying that it was a great album for its time and it's a great album now. It showed a band working well together and brought some excellent musicianship and songs to the fore.

As Turner put it, "I think *Straight Between The Eyes* was a great album. It was the first time I wrote all the songs with Ritchie, and Roger chiming in of course. I think we had it soup to nuts on that album, I really do. It's a great hard rock album. I love that album especially."

Straight Between The Eyes is an interesting album in Rainbow's overall discography in how it includes songs that cover a range of styles. There's the hard rock opening track, 'Death Alley Driver' and yet the rest of the album certainly doesn't follow along all in the sane vein. There are ballads in the form of 'Stone Cold' and 'Tearin' Out My Heart'. There are plenty of strong riff moments too such as the opening to 'Tite Squeeze' and 'Rock Fever'.

Overall, *Straight Between The Eyes* sounds right for the time in which it was made — that is to say that it doesn't break the mould and it wasn't trying to, and that there are some damn good numbers on it that provide plenty of interest.

The album didn't stand out for the wrong reasons and struck a chord with many for the right reasons; namely, the market that Blackmore had sought to target by that point in Rainbow's tenure. And really, with an opening track like 'Death Alley Driver' and Blackmore's seamless playing of a section from Bach's Toccata, what's not to love?

Discography

Personnel

Rainbow
Ritchie Blackmore – guitar
Roger Glover – bass, producer
Joe Lynn Turner – vocals
Bobby Rondinelli – drums
David Rosenthal – keyboards, orchestral arrangements

Additional Musicians
François Dompierre – orchestra conductor
Raymond Dessaint – orchestra lead

Production
Engineered by Nick Blagona (assisted by Robbie Whelan)
Recorded at Le Studio, Morin Heights, Canada
Digital mixing by Roger Glover and Nick Blagona
Digital mastering by Greg Calbi, Sterling Sound, New York

Rainbow - *Straight Between The Eyes*: In-depth

Track Listing

All tracks are written by Ritchie Blackmore, Joe Lynn Turner, and Roger Glover except where indicated.

Side One
1. Death Alley Driver (4:42) (Blackmore, Turner)
2. Stone Cold (5:17)
3. Bring On The Night (Dream Chaser) (4:06)
4. Tite Squeeze (3:15)
5. Tearin' Out My Heart (4:03)

Side Two
6. Power (4:26)
7. MISS Mistreated (4:27) (Blackmore, Turner, David Rosenthal)
8. Rock Fever (3:50) (Blackmore, Turner)
9. Eyes Of Fire (6:37) (Blackmore, Turner, Bobby Rondinelli)

By the eighties, the music business was becoming more corporate. As a consequence releases were far more generic throughout the world, with very little variation. PolyGram released Rainbow on Mercury in North America and on Polydor for the rest of the world. Most releases used picture labels utilising the album artwork, but in some territories conventional red Polydor label designs were used.

UK
Original April 1982 releases:
Polydor POLD 5056, LP
Polydor POLDC 5056, cassette

Original March 1983 CD release:
Polydor 800 028-2

Reissues:
Polydor 547 366-2, CD, 1999
Back On Black RCV025LP, LP, 2010*
*Two versions, one on black vinyl and a limited edition on brown vinyl.
Polydor 5353577, LP, 23rd February 2015

USA
Original April 1982 releases:

Mercury SRM-1-4041, LP
Mercury MCR-4-1-4041, cassette
Mercury MC8-1-4041, 8-track cartridge

Original 1983 CD release:
Polydor 800 028-2

Reissues:
Mercury 825 387-4 M-1, cassette
Polydor P2-00028, CD
Polydor 314 547 366-2, CD, 1999

Rainbow - *Straight Between The Eyes*: In-depth

Singles from the album:

Stone Cold / Rock Fever
Polydor POSP 421, 7", UK, 1982
Polydor POSPX 421, 12", UK, 1982
Mercury 76146, 7", US, 1982
(This coupling was also released throughout Europe, the Americas and Japan.)

Death Alley Driver / Tite Squeeze
Polydor 2095 472, 7", Netherlands, 1982

Death Alley Driver / Power
Polydor 7DM 0059, 7", Japan, 1982

Death Alley Driver / Eyes Of Fire
Polydor POS - 22063, 7", Bolivia, 1982

'Power' was a big radio hit in the US despite no commercial single release. However, promotional 12" copies on red vinyl were pressed up for US radio stations. To capitalise on its success the live version from *Live Between The Eyes* was also released as a promotional 12" single in 1983.

Power / MISS Mistreated
Mercury MK 204, 12", USA, 1982

Power (live version) / Power (studio version)
Mercury MK 232, 12", USA, 1983

Tour Dates

Please be aware that the following list may not be exhaustive. Conflicting accounts exist of Rainbow's tour dates. Consequently, the list here is derived from corroboration of information from posters, ticket stubs and reviews.

1982

7th May	SIU Arena, Carbondale, IL, USA
11th May	IMA Auditorium, Flint, MI, USA
13th May	Civic Centre, Grand Rapids, Lansing, MI, USA
14th May	Cobo Hall, Detroit, MI, USA
15th May	Wings Stadium, Kalamazoo, MI, USA
16th May	Coliseum, Fort Wayne, IN, USA
18th May	Sports Arena, Toledo, OH, USA
20th May	Gardens, Cincinnati, OH, USA
22nd May	Richfield Coliseum, Cleveland, OH, USA
23rd May	Convention Centre, Indianapolis, IN, USA
25th May	Holiday Star Theatre, Merrillville, IN, USA
26th May	Alumi Auditorium, Davenport, IA, USA
28th May	Westfalenhalle, Dortmund, Germany (cancelled)
29th May	Würzburg Festival, Germany (cancelled)
29th May	Iowa State Fairgrounds, Des Moines, IA, USA
2nd June	Met Centre, Minneapolis, MN, USA
4th June	Veterans Memorial Arena, Greenbay, WI, USA
5th June	Alpine Valley, Milwaukee, WI, USA
6th June	St Louis, MO, USA (cancelled)
7th June	London Gardens, London, Canada
8th June	Kitchener Memorial Auditorium, Kitchener, Canada (cancelled)
9th June	Coliseum-Exhibition Place, Toronto, Canada (cancelled)
10th June	Le Colisée. Quebec City, Canada
12th June	Verdun Auditorium, Montreal, Canada
13th June	Civic Centre, Glen Falls, NY, USA
15th June	Allentown Fairgrounds Outdoors Festival, USA

Rainbow - *Straight Between The Eyes*: In-depth

16th June	War Memorial Auditorium, Rochester, NY, USA
17th June	Memorial Auditorium, Utica, NY, USA
18th June	Coliseum, New Haven, CT, USA
19th June	Madison Square Garden, New York City, NY, USA
21st June	City Island, Harrisburg, USA
22nd June	War Memorial, Buffalo, NY, USA
23rd June	Memorial Arena, Binghamton, NY, USA
25th June	Civic Centre Providence, Rhode Island, PA, USA
26th June	Cape Cod Coliseum, South Yarmouth, MA, USA
27th June	Spectrum, Philadelphia, PA, USA
9th July	Forum, Los Angeles, CA, USA
10th July	Swing Auditorium, San Bernadino, CA, USA
11th July	Sports Arena, San Diego, CA, USA
12th July	Selland Arena, Fresno, CA, USA
14th July	Civic Auditorium, Bakersfield, CA, USA
16th July	Memorial Auditorium, Sacramento, CA, USA
17th July	Cow Palace, San Francisco, CA, USA
18th July	Centennial Coliseum, Reno, NE, USA
20th July	Capital Centre, Largo, MD, USA
22nd July	Arena, Seattle, WA, USA
23rd July	Coliseum, Portland, OR, USA
24th July	Coliseum, Portland, OR, USA
25th July	Coliseum, Spokane, WA, USA
27th July	Pacific Coliseum, Vancouver, BC, Canada
31st July	Convention Centre, Springfield, IL, USA
7th August	Municipal Coliseum, Lubbock, TX, USA
9th August	Ector County Coliseum, El Paso, TX, USA
10th August	Miland, TX, USA
11th August	Civic Centre, Amarillo, TX, USA
13th August	Busch Memorial Stadium, St Louis, MO, USA
15th August	Arrowhead Stadium, Kansas, MO, USA
?? August	Boulder, CO, USA
17th August	Sam Houston Coliseum, Houston, TX, USA
18th August	Convention Centre, San Antonio, TX, USA (filmed for official video release, *Live Between The Eyes*)

20th August	Wintergarden Ballroom, Dallas, TX, USA
?? August	Civic Centre, Lakeland, FL, USA
23rd August	New York City, NY, USA
12th October	Festival Hall, Osaka, Japan
13th October	Festival Hall, Osaka, Japan
14th October	Festival Hall, Osaka, Japan
16th October	Kaikan Daiichi Hall, Kyoto, Japan
17th October	Sun Palace, Fukouka, Japan
18th October	Shikokaido Hall, Nagoya, Japan
19th October	Shikokaido Hall, Nagoya, Japan
21st October	Budokan, Tokyo, Japan
22nd October	Budokan, Tokyo, Japan
29th October	Drammenshallen, Drammen, Oslo, Norway
30th October	Vejlby Risskov Hallen, Aarhus, Denmark
2nd November	Jäähalli, Oulu, Finland
3rd November	Jäähalli, Helsinki, Finland
5th November	Brondby Hallen, Copenhagen, Denmark
6th November	Isstadion, Stockholm, Sweden
8th November	Ernst Merck Halle, Hamburg, Germany
9th November	Deutcschland Halle, Berlin, Germany
11th November	Gruga Halle, Essen, Germany
12th November	Neckar Halle, Heidelberg, Germany
13th November	Neunkirchen Hemmerleinhalle, Nuremberg, Germany
15th November	Walter Kobel Halle, Russelheim, Germany
16th November	Ahoy, Rotterdam, Netherlands
18th November	Stadthalle, Freiburg, Germany
19th November	Rudi Sedl Mayer Halle, Munich, Germany
21st November	Patinoire Des Vernets, Geneva, Switzerland
24th November	Böblingen, Stuttgart, Germany
25th November	Eilenriederhalle, Hanover, Germany
26th November	Alsterdorfer Sporthalle, Hamburg, Germany
27th November	Forest National, Brussels, Belgium
28th November	Hippodrome, Paris, France
30th November	Plaza Toros Monumental, Barcelona, Spain
1st December	Pabellon De Deportes, Madrid, Spain

Rainbow - *Straight Between The Eyes*: In-depth

Rainbow - *Straight Between The Eyes*: In-depth

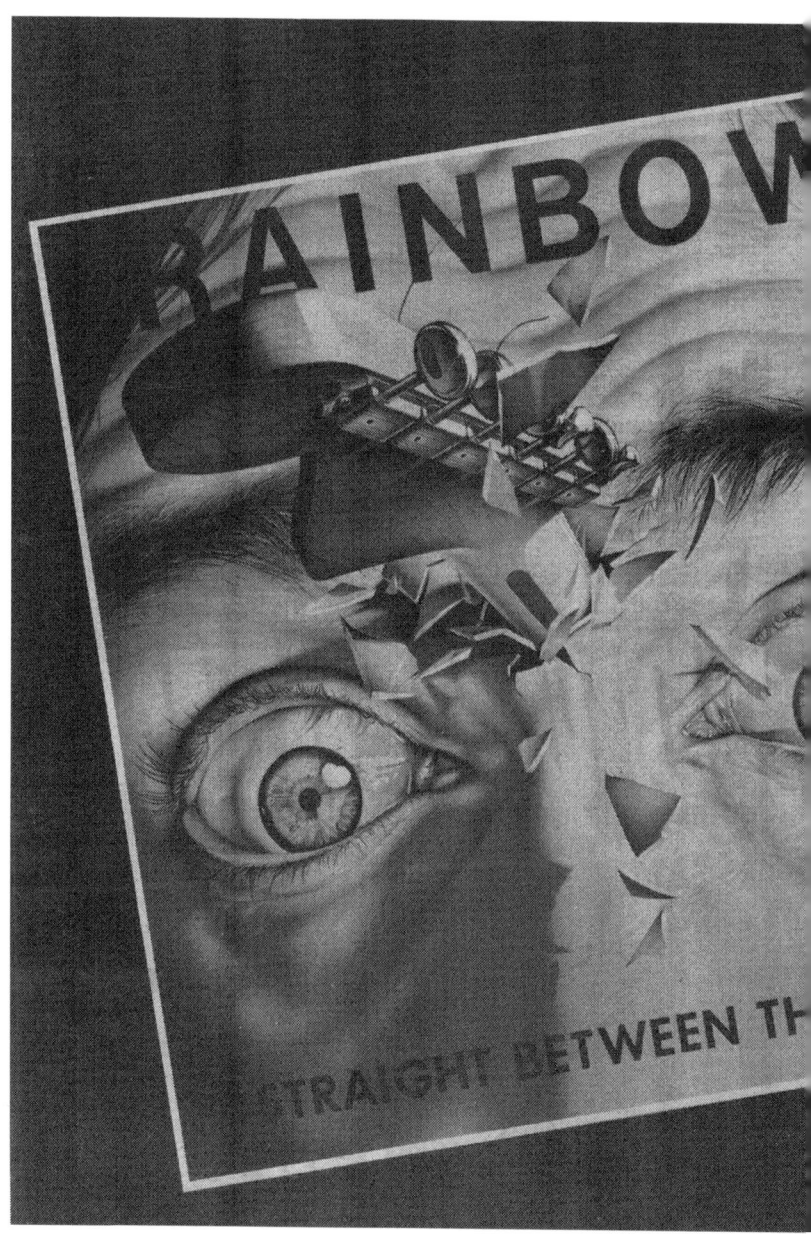

RAINBOW

THE NEW ALBUM
'STRAIGHT BETWEEN THE EYES'

INCLUDES THE HIT SINGLE
'STONE COLD'

PRODUCED BY ROGER GLOVER.

Polydor

ALSO AVAILABLE ON CASSETTE

In-depth Series

The In-depth series was launched in March 2021 with four titles. Each book takes an in-depth look at an album; the history behind it; the story about its creation; the songs, as well as detailed discographies listing release variations around the world. The series will tackle albums that are considered to be classics amongst the fan bases, as well as some albums deemed to be "difficult" or controversial; shining new light on them, following reappraisal by the authors.

Titles to date:

Jethro Tull - Thick As A Brick	978-1-912782-57-4
Tears For Fears - The Hurting	978-1-912782-58-1
Kate Bush - The Kick Inside	978-1-912782-59-8
Deep Purple - Stormbringer	978-1-912782-60-4
Emerson Lake & Palmer - Pictures At An Exhibition	978-1-912782-67-3
Korn - Follow The Leader	978-1-912782-68-0
Elvis Costello - This Year's Model	978-1-912782-69-7
Kate Bush - The Dreaming	978-1-912782-70-3
Jethro Tull - Minstrel In The Gallery	978-1-912782-81-9
Deep Purple - Fireball	978-1-912782-82-6
Deep Purple - Slaves And Masters	978-1-912782-83-3
Rainbow - Straight Between The Eyes	978-1-912782-96-3
Jethro Tull - Heavy Horses	978-1-912782-97-0
Talking Heads - Remain In Light	978-1-915246-01-1
The Stranglers - La Folie	978-1-915246-02-8